LATE NIGHT SHOPPING

www.qheartland.com

DISK
- ☐ NATO1 Nature 1 Northwoods Appliques by Cactus Punch (Winter Lodge)

HUSQVARNA VIKING FEET
- ☐ Open Toe Foot #412 27 70-45 (Chain Letter, Forget Me Not, Touch of Romance, Peak of Innocence, Sno 'n Love, Winter Lodge, Spring Cleaning)
- ☐ Open Toe Stippling Foot (Chain Letter, Forget Me Not, Touch of Romance, Grandma's Garden, Trapunto Tulip, Beginning with Finishing Touches)
- ☐ Walking Foot (Chain Letter, Forget Me Not, Peak of Innocence, Grandma's Garden, Winter Lodge, Beginning with Finishing Touches)

MISCELLANEOUS
- ☐ Buttons / 20 black 1/8" diameter (Sno 'n Love)
- ☐ Card stock paper (Winter Lodge)
- ☐ Chenille By The Inch™ by Fabric Cafe (Forget Me Not)
- ☐ Chenille Brush™ by Fabric Cafe (Forget Me Not)
- ☐ Chenille Cutting Guide™ by Fabric Cafe (Forget Me Not)
- ☐ Earthline Flowers by Julie Mullin (Beginning with Finishing Touches)
- ☐ Flora wire 26 gauge (How does your garden grow?)
- ☐ Flora Stem Wrap tape (How does your garden grow?)
- ☐ Golden Threads Quilting Paper (Chain Letter, Trapunto Tulip, Winter Lodge, Beginning with Finishing Touches)

NEEDLES
- ☐ Quilting Needle (Beginning with Finishing Touches)
- ☐ Top stitching needle (Trapunto Tulip)

NOTIONS
- ☐ Applique Pressing Sheet (Applique the Madeira Way, Sno 'n Love)
- ☐ Fabric Grips QS56
- ☐ Free-Motion Guide Grip (Beginning with Finishing Touches)
- ☐ Marking pencil (Sno 'n Love)
- ☐ Marker / permanent (Beginning with Finishing Touches)
- ☐ Marking pen / water soluble (Forget Me Not, Trapunto Tulip)
- ☐ Mat boards (large and small)
- ☐ Mini clover iron (Winter Lodge)
- ☐ Pins /Glass Head Silk 0.50mm steel shaft
- ☐ Rotary Cutter
- ☐ Stiletto STB
- ☐ Steam-A-Seam® -1/4" (How does your garden grow?)
- ☐ Spray starch (Applique the Madeira Way)
- ☐ Sulky® KK2000 Temporary Spray Adhesive (Forget Me Not, How does your garden grow?, Peak of Innocence)
- ☐ Warm & Natural® cotton batting
- ☐ Warm & Natural® polyester batting (Trapunto Tulip)

RULERS
- ☐ 2 1/2" Square Omnigrid® ruler (Spring Cleaning)
- ☐ 6" x 12" Omnigrid® ruler (Peak of Innocence)
- ☐ 6" x 24" Omnigrid® ruler
- ☐ 12 1/2" x 12 1/2" Omnigrid® ruler (Peak of Innocence)

STABILIZERS
- ☐ Fuse and Tear Stabilizer by America Sews (Applique the Madeira Way)
- ☐ Steam-A-Seam® Fusible Web (Winter Lodge)
- ☐ Steam-A-Seam® Sticky Back Fusible web (Forget Me Not)
- ☐ Sulky® Totally Stable (Winter Lodge)
- ☐ Tear Away Light Stabilizer by America Sews (Forget Me Not, Sno 'n Love)
- ☐ Wonder Under (How does your garden grow?)
- ☐ Trans Web Stabilizer (Sno 'n Love)
- ☐ Water Soluble Fusible Web (Applique the Madeira Way)

STENCILS
- ☐ ST28 tulip border stencil (Trapunto Tulip)
- ☐ ST28-5 tulip medallion stencil (Trapunto Tulip)
- ☐ ST28-6 single tulip stencil (Trapunto Tulip)
- ☐ ST-31 Poinsettia stencil (Wheel of Mystery)
- ☐ ST-S Millennium Star stencil (Winter Lodge)

TEMPLATES
- ☐ QS-31 Wheel of Mystery templates (Wheel of Mystery)
- ☐ QSK Quilter's Starter Kit templates (Chain Letter, Forget Me Not)
- ☐ SP1 Peaky and Spike templates (Touch of Romance, Trapunto Tulip, Sno 'n Love, Winter Lodge, Spring Cleaning)

THREADS
- ☐ 100% cotton thread
- ☐ Pearl Crown rayon thread (How does your garden grow?)
- ☐ Quilting Thread (Beginning with Finishing Touches)
- ☐ Serger cones thread (How does your garden grow?)
- ☐ Sulky® 12 wt. cotton thread (Forget Me Not, How does your garden grow?, Grandma's Garden, Sno 'n Love)
- ☐ Sulky® Invisible thread (Applique the Madeira Way)
- ☐ Sulky rayon 30 wt. green thread (How does your garden grow?)
- ☐ Sulky® rayon 40 wt. thread (Winter Lodge)
- ☐ Thread fuse (How does your garden grow?)
- ☐ Water Soluble Thread (Trapunto Tulip, Applique the Madeira Way)
- ☐ Wooly Nylon thread / white (How does your garden grow?)

QUILTMAKING BASICS

HOW TO USE THIS BOOK
This book contains step-by-step instructions for each design.
A. Before starting, read through entire instructions so you get an idea of the complete process.
B. There are color photos to look at if picking fabric is difficult for you. Check yardage charts for each quilt before purchasing fabric. Make sure to prepare your fabric as suggested.
C. Templates are printed in actual size at the end of this book. Acrylic templates can be purchased at your local quilt shop or from "Quilting From The Heartland", P.O. Box 610, Starbuck, MN 56381 U.S.A. 1-800-637-2541 or 1-320-239-4044

PREPARATION OF ACRYLIC TEMPLATES

Templates come with protective paper on each side; simply peel off before using. They are pink in color (so you won't lose them in your fabric) as well as transparent which allows you to take advantage of certain fabric designs.

For best accuracy while cutting with the Rotary Cutter, apply Quick Grips to each corner of the template; if it's a larger template, put one in middle along edge. Quick Grips are small circles of felt with adhesive backing. They keep templates from sliding on your fabric while cutting. Please note! If you don't put the Quick Grips on the far corners, the fabric will move when you approach corner with cutter.

PREPARATION OF FABRIC
I prefer to use 100% cotton fabric because it is lightweight making it easy to quilt through all layers of the quilt sandwich. Cotton is easy to manipulate when matching points and flexible when working with curves. If you are going to use blends, choose all fabrics of the same blend.

Separate fabrics by color and wash in cool water with a mild soap that contains no bleaching additives. If fabric still bleeds after one washing, you may consider a second wash. Line or machine dry.

Caution! If you use a steam iron when you are piecing a quilt and you haven't pre-washed the fabric, your cut pieces will shrink unevenly, making working with them difficult.

PRESS AND STARCH
I have started to use spray starch on most fabrics that go into the quilt. Starch makes cutting and sewing much easier. It also acts as a stain guard, making it easier to remove pencil lines. A light mist is adequate for most quilting projects, but if pieces are small, spray both sides of fabric.

Starch will also prevent pieces from getting pulled into needle hole when sewing.

It is cheaper to mix your own starch with equal parts of Sta-Flo liquid starch and water. Put it in a mister and lightly mist fabric before pressing it.

GRAIN OF FABRIC

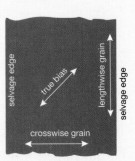

Lengthwise grain runs parallel to edge of fabric and crosswise grain runs from selvage to selvage. Both are considered to be on straight of grain. True bias is cut at a 45° angle and is stretchiest part of fabric. Avoid having bias edges of fabric on outside edge of quilt block. This will help keep quilt square; also, it will hang better if it is a wall quilt.

Occasionally I ignore this rule, especially if there is a design in the fabric that I want to capture. Because templates are transparent, you can place them in exact position before cutting. You can create some great designs, especially from border prints and stripes, but you can cut only one at a time. It will look as if a mouse has been into your

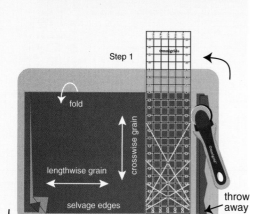

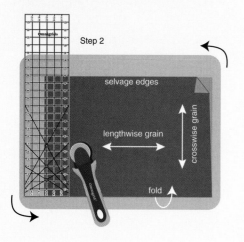

STRAIGHTENING FABRIC

Step 1. When same shapes are cut from more than one fabric used in the quilt, you can save time and accuracy by straightening more than one at the same time. Fold each fabric in half and place one on top of the other, lining up selvage edges. I like to work with folded fabric because layers seem to stabilize each other, especially if they are freshly ironed.

Place bottom edge of ruler on selvage edge. Start cutting about 1" from selvage edge going backwards off fabric. Starting in the same place, continue to cut away from yourself when trimming off uneven edges. Try not to disturb fabric after it is straightened. Bi-fold fabric on top of mat board before turning it.

CUTTING STRIPS WITH 6"X 24" RULER

Step 2. Move ruler to proper position to get width needed for strips. Cut required number of strips.

When you get more experienced with this method of straightening fabric and cutting strips, you can layer as many as six fabrics on top of each other.

If you are using a 6" x 12" Omnigrid® ruler, you will have to fold fabric in half matching selvage edges, and in half again. Note! Make sure your fabric is lying straight while cutting strips with the 6" x 12" ruler, so you don't end with zig zag strips.

After you have mastered cutting strips, it's easy to recut them into squares with a 6" x 12" ruler.

SETTING MACHINE FOR PIECING

I tell everyone that takes a class from me to make sure to sew all seams with a scant 1/4" seam allowance. This makes up for fabric used in seam line. Use scant 1/4" seam allowance for all quilt patterns that have 1/4" seam allowance included. I can't stress enough the importance of this rule.

On Husqvarna Viking Designers the scant 1/4" is found in Menu E-stitch1.

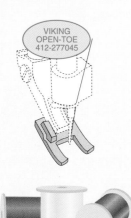

THREAD AND FEET

I prefer to use an open-toe for piecing. On an Open Toe Foot, the portion of foot directly in front of needle has been removed to give an unobstructed view of stitch.

Use 100% merc. cotton thread, size 50, to match 100% cotton fabric for care and strength. Cotton thread is strong, yet fine, for accurate piecing.

If you're using a Quilt Designer, Designer II or Designer I, don't forget to touch needle stop (⬆⬇) up/down button so needle stops in down position and presser foot comes up making it easy to pivot each time you want to readjust the fabric. It is especially nice for chain sewing because you don't have to lift the presser foot each time you feed another set of pieces.

CHAIN SEWING

I chain sew pieces together whenever possible because it saves time and thread. At beginning and end of a seam, do not back stitch or cut thread. Feed next pair of pieces under presser foot as close as possible to first pair. Continue to feed   pieces as close as possible. After all pieces have been sewn, remove chain and clip threads between pieces.

MACHINE QUILTING

Free motion quilting works best for continuous line designs, stippling, outlining flowers, and feathered designs.

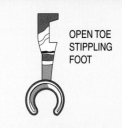

OPEN TOE STIPPLING FOOT

Before attaching Open Toe Stippling Foot, take standard ankle and presser foot off the machine. Place Open Toe Stippling Foot on the presser bar. Screw in place with the accessory thumb screw. Lower the feed teeth and set presser foot pressure to the darning position. (For Designer I, Designer II, or Quilt Designer, select the V menu, touch free motion straight stitch V1). Place the Free Motion Guide Grip on quilt. Move it forward, backward and from side to side. Move quilt or fabric at a smooth pace for even stitches. Practice controlling speed of machine on fabric scraps before starting on a finished quilt top.

FREE MOTION GUIDE GRIP

Because there is so much happening at one time, it's easy to get tense. Remember to breathe and relax when machine quilting. After all, this is fun!

Look where you're going, not at needle. If you sew too slowly, stitches will be long and if you sew too fast there will be too many stitches per inch. Practice improves your skills. Have fun with it. Just like hand quilting, every stitch won't be perfect.

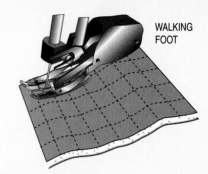

WALKING FOOT

To sew straight lines, the Walking Foot works well. It can be used for cross hatching and stitching in the ditch. The machine will do the work and you will get perfect stitches.

DOES YOUR MACHINE EAT FABRIC?

Try one or more of these tips if you are having trouble with fabric getting pulled into feed dogs.

1. Switch to a single-hole needle plate.

2. Use an anchor cloth as a leader when starting to sew. Anchor cloth is a small square of fabric folded in half. Start sewing on anchor cloth and butt the next set of pieces up to it as you sew. Beginning stitches on patchwork will be more secure and won't pull apart as easily as first stitches sewn. Cut anchor cloth from beginning of your work and sew off onto it when ending. You won't have to hold threads when starting with this method. This will also save time and thread.

3. Spray starching fabric before cutting pieces stabilizes fabric and makes stitching easy.

SILK PINS

There is a big difference in pins. Some are as big as nails. I prefer glass head silk pins with a super fine .50mm steel shaft. They are fine and never leave holes. Silk pins slide easily into fabric because of the fine shank. Silk pins are best if it is necessary to sew over pins.

STILETTO

Use a stiletto instead of your pointer finger to guide fabric in front of needle when machine piecing. You won't worry about pieces scooting to one side at end of seam, when using a stiletto.

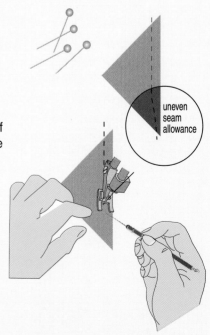

uneven seam allowance

PRESSING TECHNIQUE

It is faster to iron seams to one side, but you have more bulk in one place which makes it difficult to match some designs with triangles and hexagons. It takes more time to press seams open, but you will have a flatter quilt top making it easier to hand quilt. I will share with you which method I prefer for each quilt in this book.

There is a lot of debate about which way to iron seams when putting blocks together. There are advantages to both and I suggest you try both ways and decide for yourself which one you prefer. I don't necessarily use the fastest method, but I use the one that makes the block look best when finished. Sometimes both methods are used in the same quilt.

No matter in which direction you iron seams, always take time to finger press seams before ironing. It's much easier and you get better results when finger pressing on a hard surface. To finger press, use your pointer finger to scratch fabric in direction you want it to go as you move along seam allowance. Your finger will act as a mini iron and is often enough to do a good job. If your seam allowance does not lie flat, it's possible you didn't finger press it well. Finger pressing gives you added accuracy and speeds up ironing. It also eliminates pleats in seam wells.

After you have finger pressed seam, press it gently with a steam iron, always on wrong side. Sliding iron back and forth can cause bias edges to stretch, distorting block. Whether you press seams open or to one side, be sure to press as you go. It is harder to match unpressed seams and crossing over them can cause seam wells at intersections.

If you press seams to one side, press seams towards darker fabric whenever possible to avoid shadows under light pieces.

Place a pressing mat near your sewing machine so you don't have to leave sewing area every time you want to press a seam. I don't use the large ironing board until blocks are being connected.

Much of the time I press pieces together before starting to sew. This creates a temporary bond of pieces making it easy to keep edges aligned as they are fed under

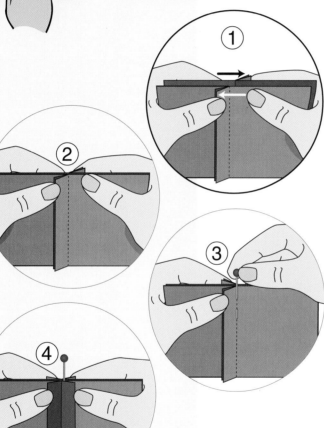

the presser foot; then, finger pinning units together is enough.

PINNING OPTIONS

I'm sharing my favorite pinning techniques. Try both and use the one that works best for you. Accurate pinning is the key to getting seams perfectly matched. Seams are pressed open with both methods. Pressed-open seams take more time but the quilt will lie flat and hang straighter.

1. To make it easier to match seams pressed open, tip seam allowance in opposite directions.

2. Slide intersection seams together. Raised area of opposing seams helps to make a perfect match.

3. Without disturbing match, tip bottom seam allowance in same direction as top seam allowance and firmly hold in place. Secure match with pin on seam line through the **block**, not the seam allowance.

4. Pin is hidden when seam allowance is flipped open. Sew slowly when sewing over pin. Seam is stitched as an opened seam. The result is a flat block when pressed.

SECOND PINNING TECHNIQUE

5. Right sides together, put two rows together. Insert a pin 1/4" from edge through top and bottom. Leave this pin standing.

6. On both sides of standing pin, insert another pin through seam allowance to hold intersection in place. Remove standing pin

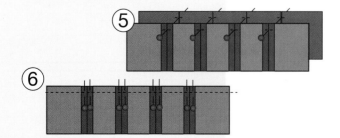

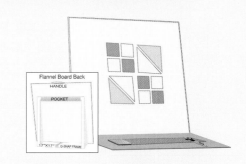

FLANNEL BOARD

Use a flannel board at cutting table when planning your next quilt. Mine has a pocket to insert a 17" x 17" Q-Snap frame to make it into an easel or a handle to hang on door or wall hook. It is easy to transport from cutting table to sewing machine or take to classes.

BORDERS

Every quilt needs one or more borders to announce its completion. Think of the border as a picture frame. If border fabric is plain, it becomes a showcase for quilting.

There can be one or more fabrics used in border which can be mitered or squared. I prefer the look of mitered corners unless there is a corner stone in the border. Corner stone can be a pieced block or a plain square.

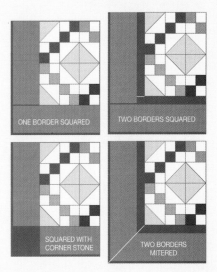

When choosing border fabric, I lay strips along edge and use what feels right. Sometimes two borders look better than one. If you use two borders, they look best if they are of different widths. You might decide to introduce a large print in border that wasn't used in quilt.

When possible, pick quilting stencil before cutting borders so you know how wide to cut strips. It's easier to mark if you purchase matching border and corner sets. Make sure width of stencil fits within border. Last 1/4" of border around outside edge should not be counted because it will eventually be covered with binding.

BORDERS WITH MITERED CORNERS

Allow extra length for mitered corners. Measure distance from top to bottom on both sides of quilt. If your measurements are different, take average length. To find out how much extra is needed, fold cut strip on the diagonal. I cut strips 6 1/2" wide for most outside borders so I need an extra 13" (6 1/2" for each end). Next, subtract from top and bottom 1/2" (1/4" seam allowance used at each end) that is used in seam.

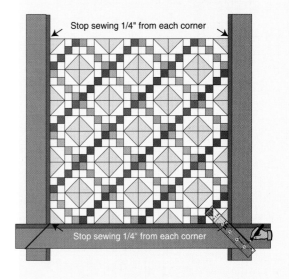

Match center of border strip to center of quilt edge. Hold in place with a pin. Insert another pin 1/4" from top and bottom end of quilt. Evenly insert more pins along edge. Sew this seam with quilt on top so intersections you want to sew over are visible. Stop sewing 1/4" from each corner on top and bottom of quilt. After all sides are attached, seams will touch in corners. Attach border on other side in same way. Repeat step to add top and bottom border.

After all four sides have been attached, iron seam allowance towards border. Cross one border over the other making a perfect 90° corner. Make a chalk line on right side of both top and bottom at a 45° angle. Match these lines and pin to hold in place. Sew this seam starting at outside point and back stitch at inside corner.

MARKING QUILTING DESIGN

Before making quilt sandwich, mark quilting designs on quilt top with a fabric marking pencil. Using pre-cut stencils is an easy, fast and economical way to transfer quilting designs. Plastic stencils have a series of slots, wide enough to allow points of pencils to mark through onto fabric. Bridges are left between slots to hold stencil together. You can join broken lines after stencil is removed to make a continuous quilting line or join them during quilting process.

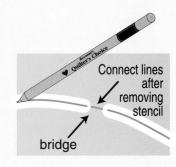

Consider open areas that need quilting. Quilting will show up more on a solid fabric than on a busy floral. If you use a fabric with very little print or even better, a solid, for back of quilt, it will be reversible. Choose stencil to complement quilt. Mark lightly through slots following lines until design is completed.

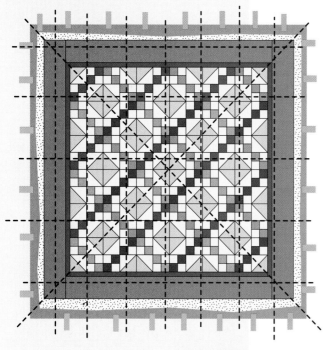

Selvage Edge
64"
45"
72"
Quilt Top
60"
45"
7"

PREPARE QUILT BACK

If light fabrics were used in quilt top, don't use dark for quilt back because it will show through. Before making quilt sandwich (front, batting, and backing) you will need to make the quilt back. The back should be 2" - 3" larger (on all four sides) than pieced top. Measure finished quilt top and add 4" - 6" to length and width. If you are making a wall quilt less than 40" wide, you won't have to sew strips of fabric together for backing. Cut length needed. If quilt is wider than 40", you will have to sew strips together. Sew seams with a 5/8" seam allowance and trim to 1/4". Iron seam open.

Measure quilt top for which you are making the back and figure out best use of fabric. Length and width of quilt will determine whether you put seam lengthwise or crosswise. Center quilt over back and leave equal amounts of extra fabric on each side.

QUILT SANDWICH

After quilting design is marked on quilt top, make a quilt sandwich by placing back of quilt on bottom with wrong side facing up. The middle is batting and pieced quilt is on top, right side facing up. Work on a table top or a tile floor if available. Smooth out and secure bottom layer in place (wrong side facing up) with masking tape. Batting and pieced top is secured in place with pins.

I prefer low-loft batting for both hand and machine quilting. It's easier to get even stitches with light batting; also, finished quilts with this batting drape nicely over beds.

Baste quilt with a large needle diagonally, vertically and horizontally. You can also pin-baste with rust proof safety pins.

BASTING QUILT SANDWICH ON TABLE TOP

Fold top of quilt in half and mark center on all four edges. Do the same with batting and backing.

Mark center of table top in three places with a toothpick held in place by masking tape. Toothpicks make a bump that can be felt through quilt sandwich layers. If quilt is longer than length of table, put a tooth pick in center of table edge.

Fold back of quilt in half, wrong sides together. Match centers of back to toothpicks on table. Unfold back with wrong side up and secure ends with masking tape. If back is longer than table, secure it with clips.

Fold batting in half and match to center bumps. Let batting drape over table top.

Fold quilt top in half, right sides together and match fold to center bumps. Unfold quilt top over table top and smooth it out. Now you are ready to baste. Start in center and work your way out. If your quilt is larger than the table top, remove clamps after it is basted and readjust quilt sandwich on table top.

Turn excess backing along outside edge over batting and baste it in place with binding clips; you have a temporary binding. This prevents batting from getting snagged during quilting process.

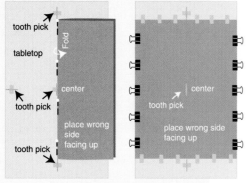

tooth pick
tabletop
Fold
center
tooth pick
place wrong side facing up

center
tooth pick
place wrong side facing up

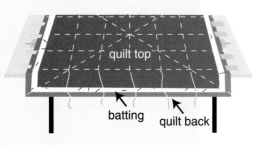

quilt top
batting
quilt back

BINDING

Machine sew with a walking foot or hand baste 1/8" from edge to keep quilt and batting from shifting while you attach binding.

Step 1. Cut enough 2" strips on the straight of grain, preferably selvage to selvage for binding. Cut strips on bias for binding curves.

Cut selvage off both ends of all strips. Position ends right sides together at a right angle and stitch as shown. Trim to 1/4" seam allowance and press seams open. Now bulk of seam will be evenly distributed.

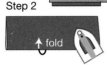

Step 1

2" wide

Step 2. Fold binding in half lengthwise, wrong sides together and press.

Step 2

fold

Step 3. Place raw edges of binding on quilt front even with edge of quilt on one of the sides. Make sure a binding seam does not fall on a corner; if it does, find a new place to start. Start sewing 7" from beginning. Sew 1/4" from edge and stop sewing 1/4" from corner of quilt edge; back stitch. Cut thread.

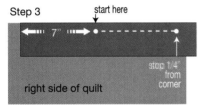

Step 3

start here

7"

stop 1/4" from corner

right side of quilt

Step 4. Turn your work and fold binding back. Binding edge and quilt edge should make a straight line when folded regardless of the angle of the quilt corner. This fold will start the miter on the corner.

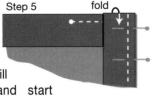

Step 4

fold

Step 5. Place your finger on first fold and flip binding down to make the second fold even with binding; this will complete miter. Pin and start sewing from the outside edge to 1/4" of next corner. Repeat steps #3 - #5 until you are around entire

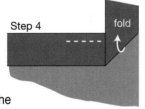

Step 5

fold

Step 6. Lay binding end down overlapping the beginning edge. Trim binding 2" past beginning edge.

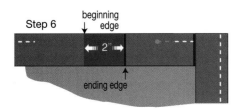

Step 6

beginning edge

2"

ending edge

Step 7. Unfold binding. Right sides together, extend both ends 1/8" (see diagram). Stitch corner to corner, like when piecing the binding strips together in step 1. Before trimming pull out straight to make sure you have sewn the end correctly.

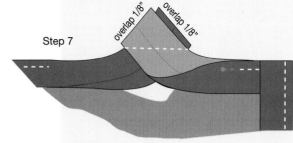

Step 7

overlap 1/8"

overlap 1/8"

Step 8. Trim to 1/4" seam allowance. Press seam open. Move binding to match quilt edge and finish sewing with 1/4" seam allowance.

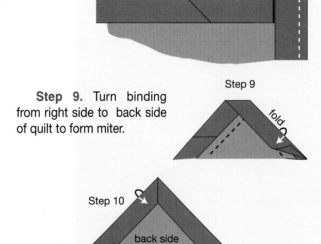

Step 8

Step 9. Turn binding from right side to back side of quilt to form miter.

Step 9

fold

Step 10

back side of quilt

Step 10. Fold other side over to complete mitered corner. Bulk in corners will automatically end opposite each other on top and bottom. Using a matching thread, hand sew with a blind stitch.

Hold binding in place with pins or binding clips as you stitch. If you use binding clips you won't have to worry about being poked with pins.

STEAM-A-SEAM® OPTION

If you are in a hurry and don't want to hand tack the binding in place this is another option. From front of quilt, press binding out over the 1/4" seam allowance. Turn quilt over to back side. Apply Steam-A-Seam 2® 1/4" (permanent) or Lite Steam-A-Seam® 1/4" (if hand stitching) to 1/4" seam allowance. Leave paper on. Press with dry iron. Take paper off. Fold binding edge down over fusible tape and cover the 1/4" seam allowance. Press with steam iron. You don't need to use pins or clips to hold in place if you still want to hand or machine stitch the binding in place.

Chain Letter yardage

Finished Wall size 57" x 57"   Queen size 108" x 120"
nine blocks   seventy-two blocks

PATTERN **291** COLOR **07**	PATTERN **292** COLOR **02**	PATTERN **296** COLOR **40**	PATTERN **300** COLOR **02**
1 yard 6 1/2 yards	1/2 yard 3 1/4 yards	1/8 yard 1 yard	

PATTERN **293** COLOR **02**	PATTERN **298** COLOR **49**	PATTERN **297** COLOR **87**	
		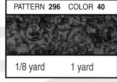	1 1/4 yards 3 1/2 yards outside outside border border & binding & binding
1/8 yard 1 yard	1/8 yard 1 yard	1/2 yard 2 yards for A's & for A's & inside border inside border	2 1/2 yards 9 1/4 yards backing backing

Age of Innocence © designed by Sharlene Jorgenson for BENARTEX INC.

designed by
Sharlene Jorgenson

pieced by
Judy Blok

machine quilted by
Jean Johnson

CHAIN LETTER
USA

SELECTING FABRIC

This quilt is a variation of the old traditional design, "The Irish Chain". The variety of light, medium, and dark textures in my new fabric collection, "Age of Innocence" helps make this an irresistible quilt. The square on point in center of each block is created with half-square triangles. Color placement of medium and dark burgundy and green prints created a ric-rac effect. Postcards from the past, featured in the outside border, gave this quilt it's name. It is great for a beginner because of it's simplicity.

Step 1. The Quilter's Starter Kit was used to make this quilt. Each block is 12" finished.

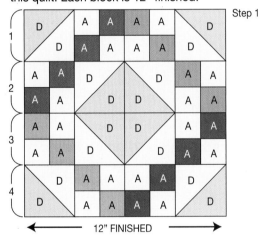

Step 1

12" FINISHED

Step 3.
Wall Size Quilt
Cut two 2" strips dark pink (A's)
Cut two 2" strips medium pink (A's)
Cut seven 2" strips beige (A's)
Cut two 2" strips light green (A's)
Cut two 2" strips of dark green (A's)

Queen Size Quilt
Cut fourteen 2" strips dark pink (A's)
Cut fourteen 2" strips medium pink (A's)
Cut fifty three 2" strips beige (A's)
Cut fourteen 2" strips light green (A's)
Cut fourteen 2" strips of dark green (A's)
See diagram for number of pieces to cut of each fabric.

SEWING INSTRUCTIONS

Step 4. Give yourself a sewing test before starting to chain sew. Place two 2" A's right sides together and sew seam with a scant 1/4" seam allowance (menu E 1 quilt stitches on Husqvarna viking Designers). You will get better results finger pressing seams open on a hard surface. Two A's sewn together should equal E template (2" x 3 1/2"). If not, adjust your seam allowance before continuing.

SHOPPING LIST
QSK Quilter's Starter Kit templates
Fabric grips
Small Rotary Cutter
Large and small mat board
6" x 24" Omnigrid® Ruler
Glass Head Silk Pins 0.05mm
Stiletto
Open Toe Foot #412 27 70-45
Walking Foot
Open Toe Stippling Foot
Golden Threads Quilting Paper
Warm & Natural cotton batting

B BEGINNER

CUTTING INSTRUCTIONS *To straighten fabric see page 4.*
Step 2. Wall size quilt
Cut four 3 7/8" strips light pink (D's)
Cut four 3 7/8" strips beige (D's)

Queen size quilt
Cut twenty seven 3 7/8" strips light pink (D's)
Cut twenty seven 3 7/8" strips beige (D's)

Place template on top of strips as shown and cut number of pieces indicated in diagram.

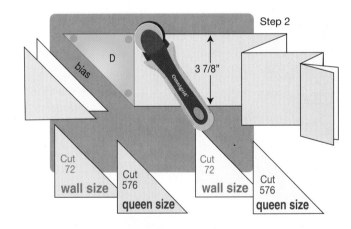

Step 2

D bias

3 7/8"

Cut 72 wall size
Cut 576 queen size
Cut 72 wall size
Cut 576 queen size

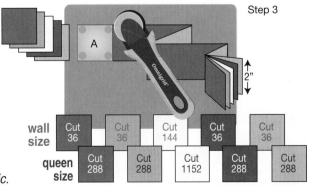

Step 3

A

2"

wall size
Cut 36 | Cut 36 | Cut 144 | Cut 36 | Cut 36

queen size
Cut 288 | Cut 288 | Cut 1152 | Cut 288 | Cut 288

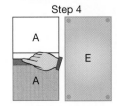

Step 4

A

A

E

Step 5

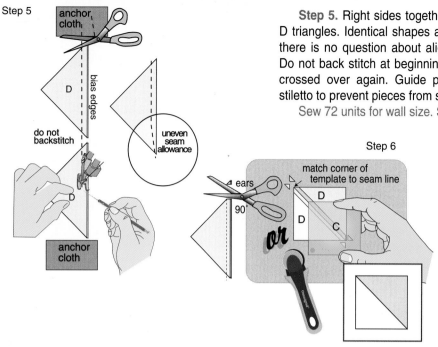

Step 5. Right sides together, join light pink D triangles to ivory D triangles. Identical shapes are easiest to sew together because there is no question about aligning them. Sew along bias edges. Do not back stitch at beginning or end of seam because it will be crossed over again. Guide pieces in front of presser foot with stiletto to prevent pieces from scooting to one side at end of seam.
Sew 72 units for wall size. Sew 576 units for queen size.

Step 6

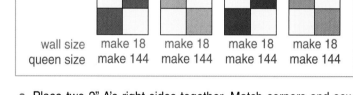

Step 6. There are two ways to remove bulk in corners. With scissors, cut at 90° angle to outside edge of block before seams are pressed open.

With second method, finger press seam open. Press with iron. Place template on top of sewn unit and match corner of template to seam line. Remove excess with rotary cutter.

Two D's sewn together must equal the 3 1/2" C square.

Step 7. Next make all four-patches needed. See diagram at right for number of each needed.

Step 7a

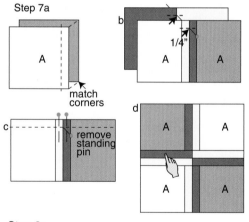

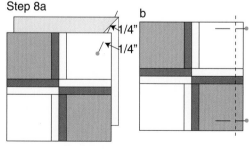

| wall size | make 18 | make 18 | make 18 | make 18 |
| queen size | make 144 | make 144 | make 144 | make 144 |

a. Place two 2" A's right sides together. Match corners and sew with a scant 1/4" seam allowance. Do not back stitch at either end of seam. Finger press seam open before pressing with an iron.

b. Place two rows of A's right sides together as shown. Insert a pin 1/4" from outside edge on seam line through top and bottom. Leave this pin standing.

c. On both sides of standing pin insert another pin to hold intersection in place. Remove standing pin. Do not back stitch when sewing seam.

d. Press seam open. See page 6 for more pinning options.

Step 8a

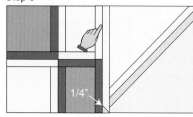

Step 8. Follow diagram in step 1 to arrange units into four rows. Starting in upper left corner of row one, connect a four-patch to a half-square unit. Make sure the units are facing the right direction. Insert a pin 1/4" from edge on top and on seam line 1/4" from edge on bottom.

b. Flip pin back into fabric. Sew directly over point pin goes into fabric. Do not back stitch.

Step 9

Step 9. Finger press seam open before pressing with an iron. Intersection should be 1/4" from edge (see arrow).

Step 10

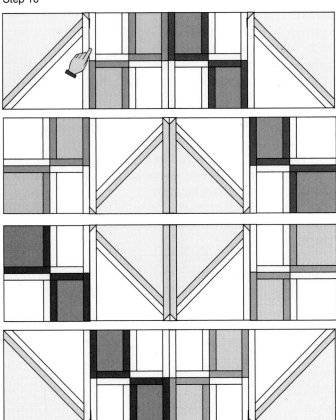

Step 10. Continue to connect units until all four rows are complete. Connect rows using same pinning technique. All seams are pressed open. Each block should measure 12 1/2".

Make nine blocks for wall quilt.

Make seventy two blocks for queen size quilt.

Step 11. Connect blocks into rows. Connect rows. Press seams open.

Step 11

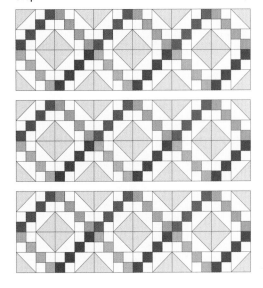

Step 12. Cut four 1" strips for wall size, 2" strips for queen size from selvage to selvage for inner border.
    Cut four 4 1/2" strips for wall size, 6" strips for queen size from selvage to selvage for outer border. Attach inner border to top and bottom edge. Press seams toward border. Attach inner border to opposite ends. Press seams toward border. Repeat this process to attach outer border.

Step 12

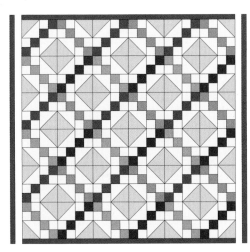

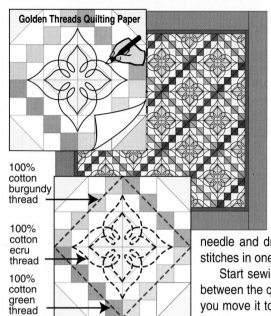

Golden Threads Quilting Paper

100% cotton burgundy thread

100% cotton ecru thread

100% cotton green thread

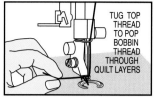

TUG TOP THREAD TO POP BOBBIN THREAD THROUGH QUILT LAYERS

See page 8 to make quilt sandwich. Cut backing and batting so that it extends 2 -3 beyond quilt top.

Trace continuous line quilting design onto Golden Thread quilting paper. For multiple copies cut several sheets to desired size. Pin together with traced design on top. Stitch with large unthreaded needle following the design to needle punch through all layers. Pin just one layer to project, quilt following the design. Remove the paper.

Read machine quilting tips on page 5 before continuing. Thread machine with a thread that's one shade darker than fabric on top and cotton thread to match back in bobbin.

Lower feed dogs. Start quilting in center. Put your quilt under needle and draw bottom thread up through fabric. Holding both threads, take a few stitches in one place. Cut loose threads.

Start sewing at a slow speed and move the quilt as you sew. You will feel tension between the quilt and needle. If you move the quilt too fast, you may break a needle. If you move it too slow your stitches may be too small. Now increase the speed of your machine and begin to move quilt at a steady, even pace.

Use a Walking Foot to stitch all straight lines. See page 9 to bind quilt.

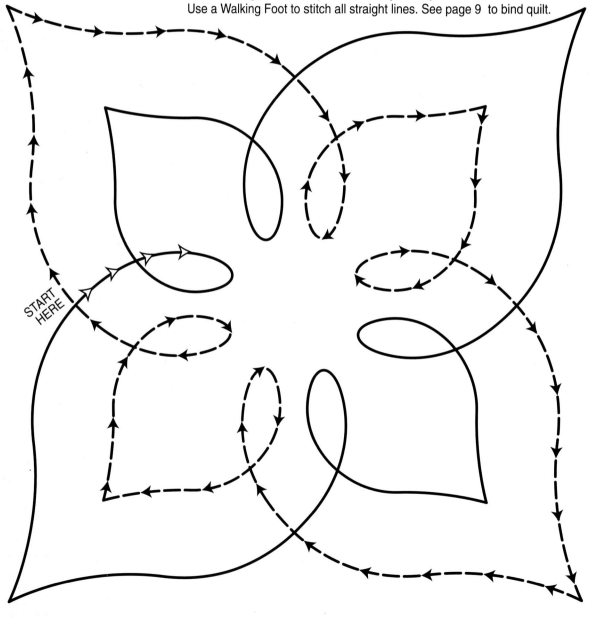

START HERE

INSIDE BORDER
QUILTING OPTION

ST15-4

ST15-3

Forget Me Not yardage
finished size 37" x 37"

1 1/2 yds. background
& pieced blocks

3/4 yd. checked fabric

2 yds. butterflies, flowers,
outside border, and binding

1/4 yd. flowers

1/4 yd. butterflies

1/8 yd. block borders

1/8 yd. block borders

2 yds. backing

**designed,
pieced, and
machine
quilted by
Fran Morgan**

Forget Me Not

SELECTING FABRIC

Fran chose bright cheerful checks for the eight pointed stars. The flower and butterfly fabrics can be solids or fabrics that read like solids. "Chenille By The Inch" is used in the center of each flower. Flowers and butterflies are appliqued with a blanket stitch using Sulky® 12 weight cotton thread. The butterflies are also embellished with chenille.

Step 1. The Quilter's Starter Kit was used to make this youth quilt. There are three different 6" finished blocks in the quilt.

Step 1

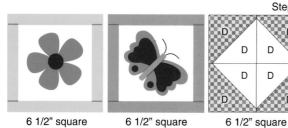

6 1/2" square   6 1/2" square   6 1/2" square

CUTTING INSTRUCTIONS

To straighten fabric see page 4.

Step 2. From checked fabric cut four strips 3 7/8" wide for D template . Cut four strips 3 7/8" wide for D template from white fabric. Place template on top of strips as shown. Flip-flop template cutting pieces as you go. Cut number of pieces indicated in diagram.

Step 2

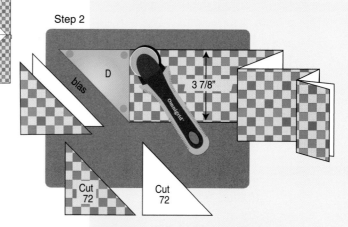

Step 3. From white cut two strips 5 1/2" wide from selvage to selvage. From these strips cut 13 white 5 1/2" squares.

Step 3

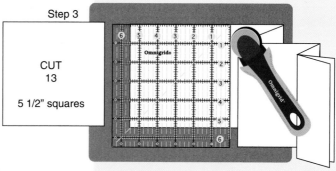

CUT
13
5 1/2" squares

Step 4. From white cut two strips 3 1/2" wide. Place template C on top of strips and cut twenty 3 1/2" squares.

Step 4

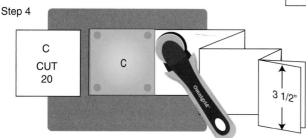

C
CUT
20

3 1/2"

Step 5. Cut one strip 6 1/2" wide x 45" long from lime green. Cut one strip 6 1/2" wide x 45" long from yellow. Cross cut these strips into 1" x 6 1/2" pieces.

Step 5

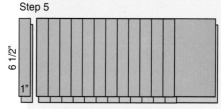

Cut 36 lime green 1"x 6 1/2" strips
Cut 16 yellow 1" x 6 1/2" strips

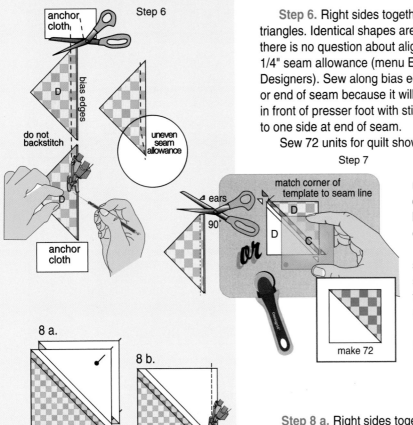

Step 6

anchor cloth

bias edges

do not backstitch

D

D

uneven seam allowance

D

anchor cloth

Step 6. Right sides together, join check D triangles to white D triangles. Identical shapes are easiest to sew together because there is no question about aligning them. Sew seams with scant 1/4" seam allowance (menu E 1 quilt stitches on Husqvarna Viking Designers). Sew along bias edges. Do not back stitch at beginning or end of seam because it will be crossed over again. Guide pieces in front of presser foot with stiletto to prevent pieces from scooting to one side at end of seam.

Sew 72 units for quilt shown on page 16.

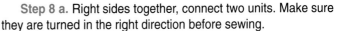

Step 7

ears

90°

match corner of template to seam line

D

D   C

or

make 72

Step 7. There are two ways to remove bulk in corners. With scissors, cut at 90° angle to outside edge of block before seams are pressed open.

With second method, finger press seam open. Place template on top of sewn unit and match corner of template to seam line. Remove excess with rotary cutter.

Two D's sewn together must equal the 3 1/2" C square.

8 a.

8 b.

8 c.

Make 36

1/4"

Step 8 a. Right sides together, connect two units. Make sure they are turned in the right direction before sewing.

8 b. To make a perfect intersection, insert pin 1/4" from edge on seam line through top and bottom. Leave this pin standing. Insert another pin at an angle as shown and remove standing pin. Do not back stitch at beginning or end of seam.

8 c. Finger press seam open before pressing with an iron. Intersection should be 1/4" from edge.

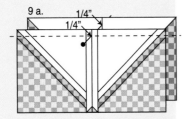

9 a.   1/4"
1/4"

Step 9a. Place two units made in step 8 right sides together. Insert a pin 1/4" from outside edge on seam line through top and bottom row. Leave this pin standing. On both sides of standing pin insert another pin to hold intersection in place. Remove standing pin before sewing.

9 b. Finger press seam open before pressing with an iron.

9 c. Notice intersections are 1/4" from edge.

9 b.

9 c.

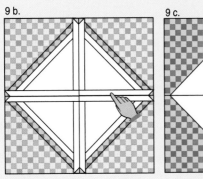

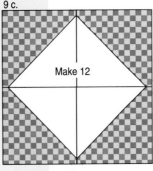

Make 12

6 1/2" square

Step 10. Trace flower, butterfly, butterfly wing and butterfly dot to web side of light Steam-A-Seam® fusible web. Cut apart leaving small margin beyond drawn lines and peel off liner. Stick patterns to wrong side of appropriate fabric. Cut apart following traced lines.

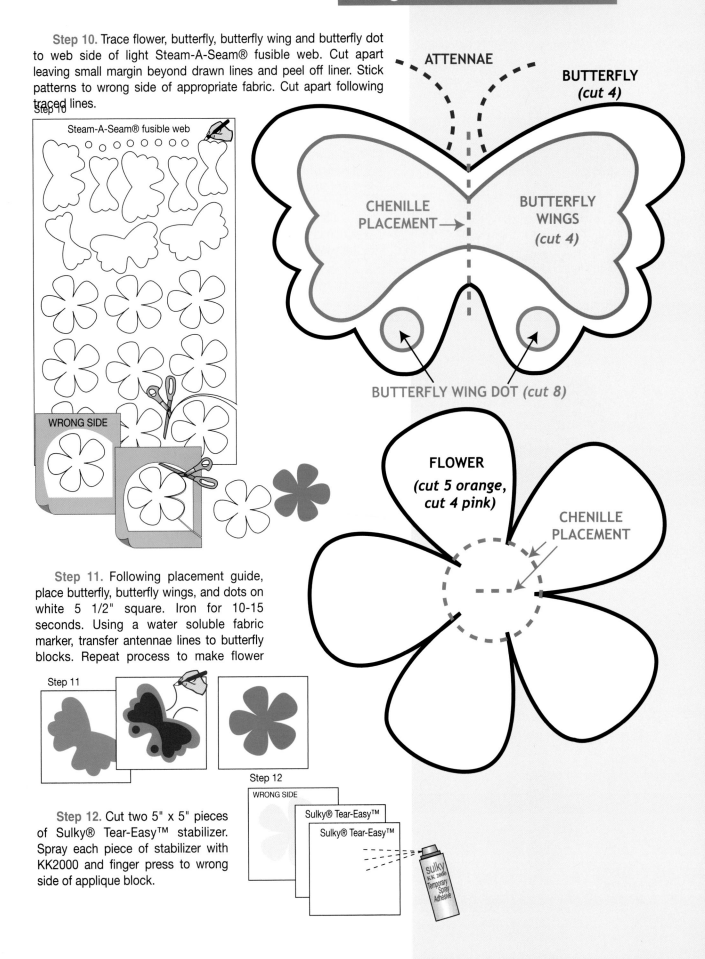

ATTENNAE

BUTTERFLY
(cut 4)

Step 10

Steam-A-Seam® fusible web

WRONG SIDE

CHENILLE
PLACEMENT →

BUTTERFLY
WINGS
(cut 4)

BUTTERFLY WING DOT *(cut 8)*

FLOWER
*(cut 5 orange,
cut 4 pink)*

CHENILLE
PLACEMENT

Step 11. Following placement guide, place butterfly, butterfly wings, and dots on white 5 1/2" square. Iron for 10-15 seconds. Using a water soluble fabric marker, transfer antennae lines to butterfly blocks. Repeat process to make flower

Step 11

Step 12

WRONG SIDE

Sulky® Tear-Easy™

Sulky® Tear-Easy™

Step 12. Cut two 5" x 5" pieces of Sulky® Tear-Easy™ stabilizer. Spray each piece of stabilizer with KK2000 and finger press to wrong side of applique block.

Sulky
K.K 2000
Temporary
Spray
Adhesive

Step 13

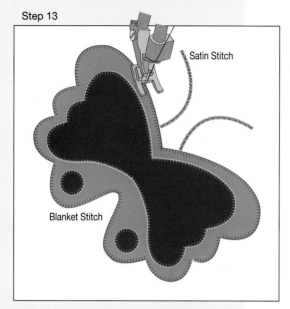

Satin Stitch

Blanket Stitch

Step 13. Use a matching Sulky® rayon thread to sew the blanket stitch (on Husqvarna Viking Designers select menu F, stitch 15, 2.5 length, 2.5 width) along the edges of butterfly wings and dots. Use open toe foot for better visibility and the tunnel on underside of this foot feeds smoothly over stitches. On Husqvarna Viking Designers touch ⊕ needle stop up/down button so needle stops in down position and presser foot comes up making it easy to pivot each time you want to readjust the fabric. Blanket stitch along edges of all flowers.

Satin stitch (on Husqvarna Viking select menu F, stitch 3) antennae using Sulky® 40 wt. rayon thread following the transferred lines. Remove Tear Easy™. Repeat until you have

Step 14

CHENILLE BY THE INCH™

Fabric Café

Step 14. Remove tear-away backing from Chenille By The Inch™. Using the Chenille Cutting Guide™, cut between stitching lines with a rotary cutter, Cut into strips.

Sew in center of Chenille By The Inch™ with straight stitch following chenille placement lines on flower and butterfly patterns.

Step 15. On pink flower (5 1/2" blocks) sew yellow 1" x 6 1/2" strips to top and bottom of block with scant 1/4" seam allowance. Trim off excess. Press seams towards 1" strips. Add 1" strips to both sides of blocks. Press seams towards strips. Repeat until you have framed four pink flower blocks with yellow. Frame five orange flower blocks with lime green strips. Frame the butterfly blocks with lime green strips.

Step 15

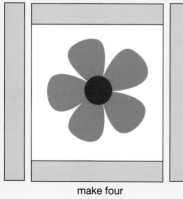

make four
6 1/2" square

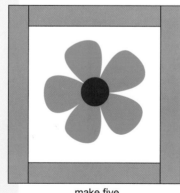

make five
6 1/2" square

make four
6 1/2" square

ASSEMBLE QUILT TOP

Step 17. Arrange blocks into seven rows. The top and bottom rows are made with units in step 8c and C squares. The beginning and end of rows 2-7 also use units made in step 8c.

Right sides together sew units together with triangles on top so intersection you want to sew over is visible. This gives you a perfect point on right side. Press seams open.

Connect the rows and press seams open.

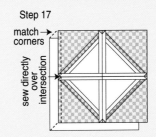

Step 17

match → corners

sew directly over intersection

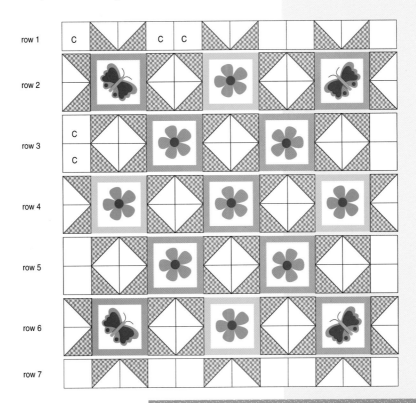

row 1

row 2

row 3

row 4

row 5

row 6

row 7

Step 18. Fran cut four 1 1/2" strips for outside border. Attach outside border to top and bottom of quilt. Press seams towards the border. Attach border to both sides. See page 8 to make quilt sandwich.

The diagram gives you quilting ideas. Stitch 1/4" inside each triangle. The white background and outside border is filled with meandering. To attach binding see page 9.

Step 19. Using a spray bottle with distilled water, dampen sewn Chenille By The Inch" strips. Brush vigorously to fluff the chenille. Enjoy your finished quilt.

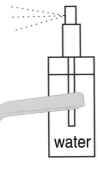

water

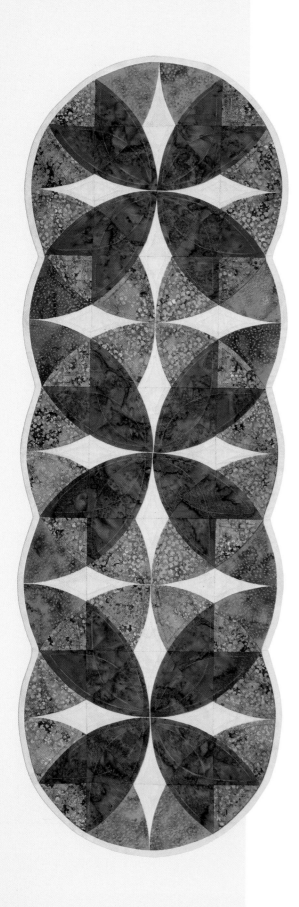

Wheel of Mystery Table Runner
Yardage
finished size
12" x 36"

- 1/8 yd. green
- 1/2 yd. purple
- 1/4 yd. yellow
- 1/2 yd. magenta

designed by
Sharlene Jorgenson

pieced by
Phyllis Peterson

machine quilted by
Sharlene Jorgenson

Wheel of Mystery

Step 1. The table runner pictured on page 22 made with the Wheel of Mystery template set has only three shapes. Each block is a 6" square finished and 6 1/2" square unfinished. Partial blocks create the scalloped border.

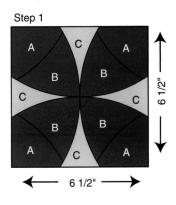

Step 1

6 1/2"

6 1/2"

CUTTING INSTRUCTIONS

Prepare fabric as suggested on page 3. Look at page 4 for instructions to straighten fabric and cut strips.

Step 2.
■ Cut strips going from selvage to selvage. Arrows on pieces A, B, & C indicate straight of grain.
■ Cut strips for template A 3" wide.
■ Cut strips for templates B & C, 3 1/2" wide.

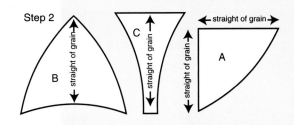

Step 2

B

C

A

straight of grain

Step 3.
■ Cut one strip 3 1/2" wide from pink.
■ Cut one strip 3 1/2" wide from purple.
■ Cut two strips 3 1/2" wide from green.
Bifold 3 1/2" strips on a small mat board to make it easy to turn the board as you're cutting around the template. Place template B on top of the strips. To save time, cut pieces from all three colors at the same time. Flip-flop the template as you work your way across the strips. There is very little waste. Each strip yields 15 B's. Cut the pieces needed of each color.

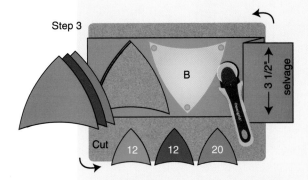

Step 3

B

3 1/2"

selvage

Cut   12   12   20

Step 4.
■ Cut two gold strips 3 1/2" wide.
Bifold strips on a small mat board. Flip-flop template C as shown, cutting pieces as you work your way across the strips. Turn the board as you cut around the template. Each strip yields 25 C's. See diagram for number of pieces needed.

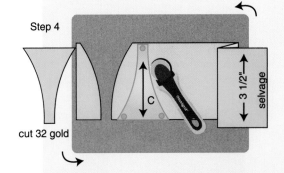

Step 4

C

3 1/2"

selvage

cut 32 gold

Step 5.
■ Cut two strips 3" wide from the purple.
■ Cut one strip 3" wide from the green.
The straight edges of the A piece form the corner of each block. To keep the block from getting distorted, place the straight edge of template A parallel to the straight edges of the strips.

Bifold the 3" strips on a small mat board base. Flip-flop template, cutting pieces as you work your way across the strips. There will be very little waste. Each strip yields 22 A's. See diagram for number of pieces needed.

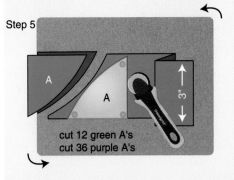

Step 5

A

A

3"

cut 12 green A's
cut 36 purple A's

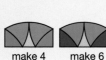

SEWING INSTRUCTIONS FOR TABLE RUNNER

Step 6. Arrange pieces on a flannel board before starting to sew. Blocks in the diagram are separated so it is easier to follow. The scalloped edge is made up of partial blocks.

Step 7. The center of the table runner is made up of two different blocks and the scalloped edge is made up of three different partial blocks.

Step 7

make 2   make 4   make 6   make 2   make 3

CONNECT THE A'S AND B'S

Step 8. To mark the center of curved edge of A piece, fold it in half diagonally and cut a small notch. Don't cut it so big that it goes into the 1/4" seam allowance. Fold B in half and cut a notch on curved edge.

Step 8

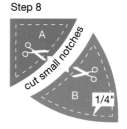

A

cut small notches

B   1/4"

Step 9

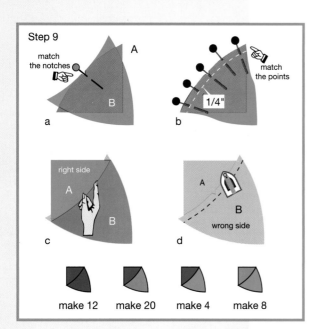

match the notches

A

B

a

match the points

1/4"

b

right side

A

B

c

A

B

wrong side

d

make 12   make 20   make 4   make 8

Step 9a. With right sides together and the B on top, match the notches. Insert a pin to secure.

Step 9b. Match points. Put a pin at each end and another one in between. This is a gentle curve so it is easy to sew. Sew all seams with a scant 1/4" seam allowance.

Step 9c. On right side, finger press seam towards A piece.

Step 9d. On wrong side, press seam allowance towards A.

Step 10

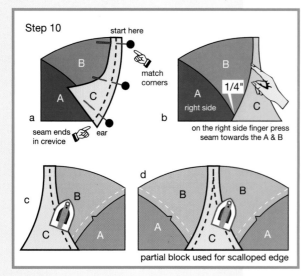

start here

B

A   C

match corners

a

seam ends in crevice   ear

B

A   C

right side

1/4"

b

on the right side finger press seam towards the A & B

c

B

C   A

d

B   B

A   C   A

partial block used for scalloped edge

Step 10a. Right sides together, place a C on top of an A/B unit. Match top corners. Match ears at end of seam. Start sewing at the top. Do not back stitch at beginning or end of seam. Use a stiletto to guide fabric. Seam will end in crevice.

Step 10b. On right side, finger press seam allowance away from C. The intersection should be 1/4" away from edge.

Step 10c. On the wrong side, press with an iron.

Step 10d. With the C on top, add another A/B unit. Press out seam allowance. This completes a partial block for scalloped edge. Look at step 7 to see how many to make.

Step 11. Place two C's right side together and chain sew five pairs together. Press seams open.

Step 12a. Right sides together, add C's to the partial block. Insert a pin 1/4" from the edge on the seam line through top and bottom. Leave this pin standing.

Step 12b. On both sides of standing pin, insert another pin. Remove the standing pin. Pin at both ends. Match ears at both ends. Move curves into a match and insert more pins. Sew with C's on top. Do not back stitch. The seam begins & ends in crevice.

Step 13. Press seam towards the A/B units.

To finish the block add another partial block. Sew seam with C's on top. Use pinning techniques in step 12a and b. Press seam allowance as shown in diagram.

Look at step 7 to see how many blocks to make.

Step 14. Arrange blocks into rows and sew together.

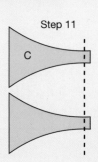

Step 11

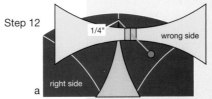

Step 12

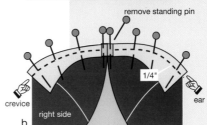

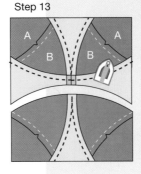
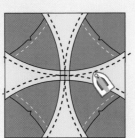

Step 13

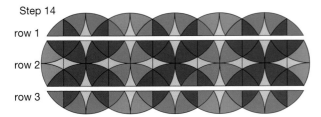

Step 14

row 1

row 2

row 3

Step 15. Place row 1 on bottom, right side up. Put row 2 to be added wrong side up. At both intersections, insert a pin 1/4" from edge on seam line through top and bottom. Because there is a lot of bulk at this intersection, I decided to fold back the seam allowance on the top side.

On both sides of the standing pin, insert another pin. Remove the standing pin. Sew directly over the intersection.

Step 15

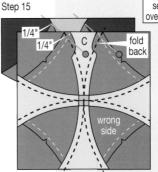
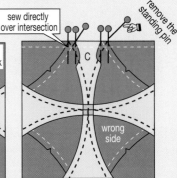

Step 16. Connect rows. Use pinning techniques in step 15. See page 8 to make the quilt sandwich.

Step 17. Place stencil ST-31 over center of each flower. Use a marking pencil that best shows on your fabric. After flowers are quilted, the remaining pieces will be quilted 1/4" from the edge.

Now that all of the secrets have been revealed about this design, I hope I've given you confidence to take a chance at creating your own Wheel of Mystery quilt.

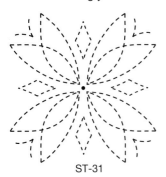

ST-31

Step 17

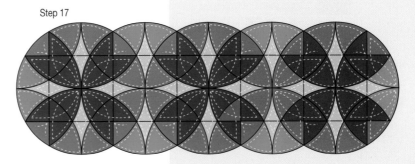

How does your garden grow? yardage

Finished size: 37" x 37"

- 1/4 yd. yellow for sun
- 1/4 yd. green for grass
- 1 yd. blue for sky background
- 1/4 yd. medium green for stems and leaves
- 1/4 yd. dark green for stems and leaves
- 1/3 yd. each of three fabrics for dimensional flowers
- 1/3 yd. white for picket fence
- 1 1/8 yd. backing

designed and serged by
Carol Vealey

machine quilted by
Linda Tailor

How does your garden grow?

ABOUT THIS QUILT

Step by step Carol takes you on an adventure that will teach you how to use your serger as you make dimensional flowers and embellishments for your garden. Each part of the quilt is made with different techniques, experimenting with decorative threads and wire.

CUTTING INSTRUCTIONS

Step 1.
Cut six 4" squares of one flower fabric (blue)
Cut one 4" square of batting
Cut six 1 1/2" x 22" strips for stems (green)
Cut one strip 3" x 44" gathered rose
Cut one strip 3" x 44" for large carnation
Cut two strips 2" x 44" for small carnations
Cut four strips 2" x 44" for white fence
Cut 2 strips 2" x 44" for wired flowers
Cut one strip 2" x 44" dark green for leaves
Cut one piece 29" x 31" for blue sky background
Cut green grass from pattern
Cut yellow sun from pattern

SHOPPING LIST

4 Serger cones thread-good quality/blender color
3 Sulky rayon 30 wt. green thread
1 Spool Thread Fuse
2 Spools Sulky 12 wt. thread (to coordinate with flower fabric)
1- 2 Spools white Wooly Nylon thread
2 Spools Pearl Crown rayon thread (to coordinate with flower fabric)
1/2 yd. Wonder Under
Flora Wire 26 gauge
Flora Stem Wrap Tape
Warm & Natural® cotton batting
1/4" Steam-A-Seam®
Rotary cutter
6" x 24" Omnigrid® ruler
KK 2000 spray adhesive
Large and small mat board

I INTERMEDIATE

BLUE FOLDED FLOWER - 4 THREAD
TECHNIQUE: MAKING WRAPPED CORNERS

Step 2. Set serger for 4 thread overlock (Husqvarna Viking 936 Serger owners - see info display). Thread with serger cone thread.

Step 3. Put two 4" squares right sides together. Place a 4" square of batting on the bottom. Serge while cutting off a blade's width. Start 1 1/4" before corner. Have needles raised in highest position and place fabric under foot to start. Serge off the end about 6". Cut tail close to corner of flower.

Step 4. Fold back corner the width of serged seam. Drop presser foot. Serge while cutting a blade's width over the fold and continue to next corner. Serge off a 6" tail. Cut tail to corner of flower. Repeat for all corners.

Step 5. On the fourth edge you need to leave an opening in the middle for turning it inside out. Fold back corner the width of serged seam. Drop presser foot. Serge a cutting blade's width over the fold and stop after you have serged 1". Lift presser foot. Turn hand wheel to lift needle to highest position. Gently tug on needle threads just above needles. Slide fabric back and off to side. Drop presser foot. Serge 6" tail away from flower. Turn flower right side out through opening.

Use a blunt object to push out corners when turning the flower to the right side.

Step 6. Place a strip of 1/4" Steam A Seam® in opening and press with iron.

Step 7. This flower will be folded diagonally. Do not fold it exactly in half so it will look like an imaginary wild flower. Scrunch it in the middle and hand sew to hold in place. A long chain of serging (see step 26) will be tacked by hand to simulate a stamen in the center.

This technique can be used to turn crisp corners on pillow tops, pillow cases, and collars.

Step 2

Auto A1   Woven med
4 thread overlock
Length :2.5 Diff :1.0
N CD N   N N N N –

Info display
on a
Husqvarna Viking
936 Serger

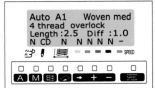
Step 3

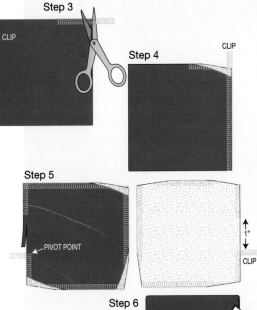
Step 4
CLIP
CLIP
Step 5
PIVOT POINT
1"
CLIP
Step 6
1/4" STEAM-A-SEAM

Step 7

Step 8

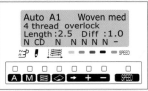

Info display on a
HusqvarnaViking 936 Serger

MAKING STEMS -4 THREAD
TECHNIQUE: TURNING STEMS WITH SERGED TAIL.

Step 8. Set serger for 4 thread overlock (Husqvarna Viking 936 Serger owners - see info display). Thread with serger cone thread.

Step 9

FOLD   WRONG SIDE

Step 9. The serger can actually serge on air. First serge a tail longer than the stem you are going to make. Right sides together, fold green stem (1 1/2" x 22") in half lengthwise matching raw edges. Tuck serged tail into the fold making sure you serge the edges together without catching the tail. Serge off the end.

Step 10

RIGHT SIDE   WRONG SIDE

MAKE SIX

Step 10. Hold onto the tail as you gently turn the stem inside out. Repeat and make 6 stems.
This technique has many uses - for example, straps on garments.

Step 11

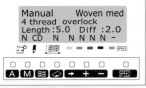

Info display on a
HusqvarnaViking 936 Serger

ROSE FLOWERS - 4 THREAD
TECHNIQUE: ADJUSTING DIFFERENTIAL TO GATHER FABRIC

Step 11. Set serger to 4 thread overlock (Husqvarna Viking 936 Serger owners - see info display). Adjust stitch length to 5.0 and differential to 2.0 width 7.0. The feed teeth pulls the fabric in faster than it lets it out. **Remember, the longer the stitch length and the higher the differential, the tighter it gathers!**

Step 12

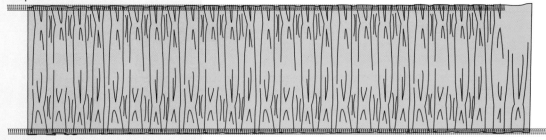

Step 12. Serge on edge of 3" x 44" strip. Hold back fabric with your hand behind serger to encourage fabric to gather more. Repeat and serge on opposite edge.
This technique could be used to make puffing for heirloom or an insert in a pillow or garment.

Step 13

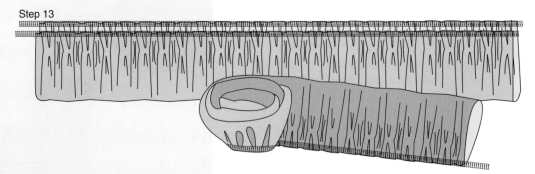

Step 13. Fold the long strip wrong sides together matching the serged edges. Roll up to form a rose and stitch together by hand with needle and thread. Rose will be attached to a stem on the quilt by hand after completing step 39.
This rose could also be used to decorate a hat.

BLUE FLOWER- 3 THREAD
TECHNIQUE: THREE THREAD WIDE WITH DECORATIVE THREADS.
LEARN TRICKS TO TURN PERFECT CORNERS.

Step 14

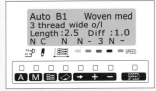

Info display on a
HusqvarnaViking 936 Serger

Step 14. Set serger for three thread wide (Husqvarna Viking 936 Serger owners - see info display). Thread upper and lower looper with Pearl Crown Rayon decorative thread and regular/cone thread in left needle. The loopers allow us to use heavier thread because we are not restricted by the eye of the needle. **Hint- when using heavier decorative threads you may need to lower the upper and lower looper tensions.**

Step 15

Step 15. Place two 4" squares wrong sides together. Do not cut fabric, use your blade as a guide. Serge to the very edge of fabric and stop. Raise needle to highest position. Raise presser foot. The trick to getting a perfect square corner is to pull needle thread down just a hair to allow you to slide the fabric off the stitch finger. Reposition fabric for turning the corner; here is where most people make a mistake. Put needle almost touching the edge of the fabric. (When you slide the fabric off the stitch finger you create excess thread length.) So before serging the next edge, pull excess thread back through the needle and loopers. Repeat until you have sewn all four edges. Before attaching this flower to the quilt, the center will be scrunched and secured with needle and thread. A button will be added in the center when it is attached to a stem with needle and thread.

This technique is a great finish for placemats, coasters, and vests.

CARNATION - 3 THREAD
TECHNIQUE: USE SERGED TAIL FOR GATHERING

Step 16

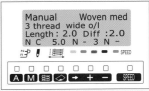

Info display on a
HusqvarnaViking 936 Serger

Step 16. Set seger for 3 thread wide overlock (Husqvarna Viking 936 Serger owners - see info display). Set stitch length 2.0 stitch width 5.0. Thread upper and lower looper with 12 wt. cotton thread. Put serger cone thread in needle.

Step 17

Step 17. Serge a long tail. Fold 3" x 44" strip in half, wrong sides together. Tuck tail into fold. Serge together without catching the tail. Cut a blade's width.

Use the tail to gather up the flower.

PICKET FENCE - 3 THREAD
TECHNIQUE: ROLLED EDGE WITH WOOLLY NYLON THREAD

Step 18

Info display on a
HusqvarnaViking 936 Serger

Step 18. Set serger for 3 thread rolled edge (Husqvarna Viking 936 Serger owners - see info display). In order to make a pretty rolled edge you need to tighten the lower looper tension so it wraps all the way around. Adjust tension N-1-8. Thread upper looper with woolly nylon. Thread lower looper with serger cone thread or woolly nylon. Unlike 3 thread overlock you will use a narrow stitch, so use the right needle. **Remember to remove your stitch finger.** This is the stitch you see in dinner napkins.

Step 19

RIGHT SIDE

Step 19. With wrong sides together, fold 2" x 44" strips lengthwise. Cut a blades width when serging. Repeat to make all strips needed for picket fence.

Step 20. Take two strips and cut in half (four 22" strips). Fold and make miters for prairie points. Other two strips will be used for rails.

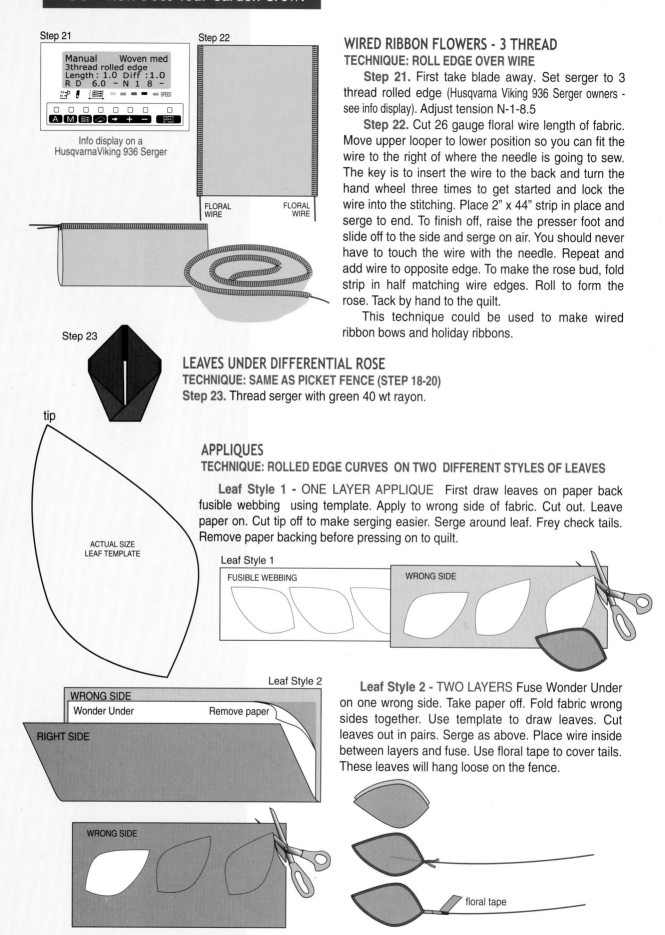

Step 21

Manual   Woven med
3thread rolled edge
Length : 1.0 Diff :1.0
R D   6.0 – N 1 8 –

SPEED

A M

SPEED

Info display on a
HusqvarnaViking 936 Serger

Step 22

FLORAL
WIRE

FLORAL
WIRE

Step 23

tip

ACTUAL SIZE
LEAF TEMPLATE

WIRED RIBBON FLOWERS - 3 THREAD
TECHNIQUE: ROLL EDGE OVER WIRE

Step 21. First take blade away. Set serger to 3 thread rolled edge (Husqvarna Viking 936 Serger owners - see info display). Adjust tension N-1-8.5

Step 22. Cut 26 gauge floral wire length of fabric. Move upper looper to lower position so you can fit the wire to the right of where the needle is going to sew. The key is to insert the wire to the back and turn the hand wheel three times to get started and lock the wire into the stitching. Place 2" x 44" strip in place and serge to end. To finish off, raise the presser foot and slide off to the side and serge on air. You should never have to touch the wire with the needle. Repeat and add wire to opposite edge. To make the rose bud, fold strip in half matching wire edges. Roll to form the rose. Tack by hand to the quilt.

This technique could be used to make wired ribbon bows and holiday ribbons.

LEAVES UNDER DIFFERENTIAL ROSE
TECHNIQUE: SAME AS PICKET FENCE (STEP 18-20)
Step 23. Thread serger with green 40 wt rayon.

APPLIQUES
TECHNIQUE: ROLLED EDGE CURVES ON TWO DIFFERENT STYLES OF LEAVES

Leaf Style 1 - ONE LAYER APPLIQUE First draw leaves on paper back fusible webbing using template. Apply to wrong side of fabric. Cut out. Leave paper on. Cut tip off to make serging easier. Serge around leaf. Frey check tails. Remove paper backing before pressing on to quilt.

Leaf Style 1

FUSIBLE WEBBING

WRONG SIDE

Leaf Style 2

WRONG SIDE

Wonder Under   Remove paper

RIGHT SIDE

WRONG SIDE

Leaf Style 2 - TWO LAYERS Fuse Wonder Under on one wrong side. Take paper off. Fold fabric wrong sides together. Use template to draw leaves. Cut leaves out in pairs. Serge as above. Place wire inside between layers and fuse. Use floral tape to cover tails. These leaves will hang loose on the fence.

floral tape

CONSTRUCTION

Step 24. Cut light blue for sky 29 1/2" x 31". Make pattern for grass. Cut grass from green fabric. Place right side of grass to wrong side of sky. Follow top edge of grass with water soluble marker. Remove grass.

Make pattern for sun. Cut sun out of yellow fabric. Place right side of sun to wrong side of sky in upper right corner. Follow edge with water soluble marker. Remove sun.

Step 25. Draw lines to radiate from sun on wrong side. Spray wrong side of grass with KK 2000. Place wrong side of grass to right side of sky. Put 1/4" Steam-A-Seam strips to back side of stems. Arrange stems in flower garden with bottoms tucked under grass. Press with iron to hold stems in place. Stems look better cut different lengths. On wrong side of quilt draw center line of each stem with wash away marker for ease of stitching.

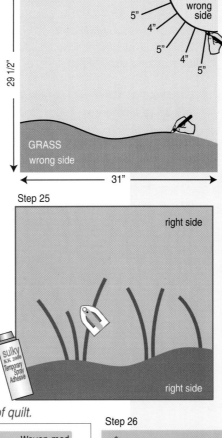

SERGING OF BACKGROUND

Note: All serging will be done from wrong side of quilt.

Step 26. Set serger to Chainstitch (Husqvarna Viking 936 Serger owners - see info display). Change tension of chainstitch lower looper to 2 or 2.5. Chain stitch in center of green stems with green 30 wt rayon thread in needle and looper. Stitch on wrong side of quilt.

Change looper thread to canary yellow pearl crown rayon and regular thread in needle to chainstitch sun rays. Using edge of foot as a guide, start chain stitching on the right side of line. Taper to a point as you near the end. To pivot at point of rays, carefully lift needle almost out of fabric. Readjust and chainstitch back towards the sun using edge of foot as a guide along line.

Spray wrong side of sun with KK 2000. Right side up, place sun to upper left side of sky on right side of fabric.

While yellow thread is still in serger, make extra chain for center of flower made in step 7.

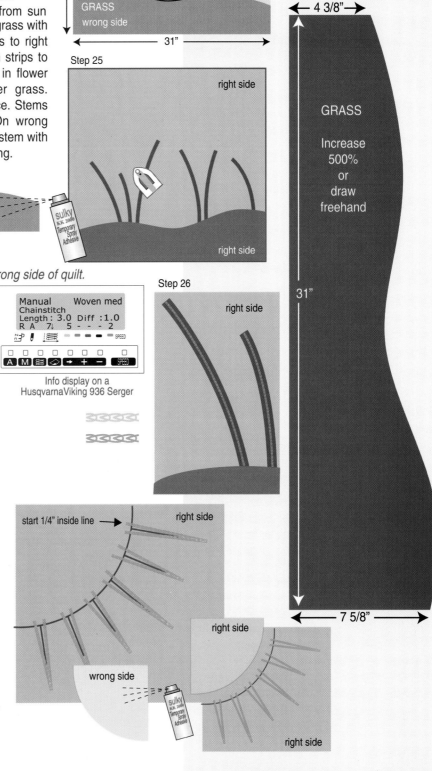

Step 24

wrong side

SUN
wrong side

4"
5"
4"
5"
4"
5"

29 1/2"

GRASS
wrong side

31"

8"

SUN
Increase
500% or
draw
freehand

8"

4 3/8"

GRASS
Increase
500%
or
draw
freehand

31"

7 5/8"

Step 25

right side

right side

wrong side

Step 26

right side

right side

Manual	Woven med
Chainstitch	
Length : 3.0	Diff :1.0
R A 7↓	5 - - 2

A M + − SPEED

Info display on a
HusqvarnaViking 936 Serger

start 1/4" inside line →

right side

wrong side

right side

right side

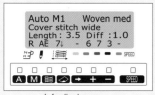

Auto M1   Woven med
Cover stitch wide
Length : 3.5 Diff :1.0
R AE 7↓ - 6 7 3 -

Info display on a
Husqvarna Viking 936 Serger

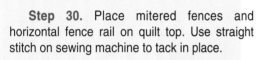

Manual   Woven med
Cover stitch wide
Length : 3.0 Diff :1.0
R AE 7↓ - 6 7 3 -

Info display on a
Husqvarna Viking 936 Serger

Step 27. Set serger to Cover Stitch Wide to attach the sun (Husqvarna Viking 936 Serger owners - see info display). Start serging on an anchor cloth. Serging on wrong side of quilt, follow your marked line on round edge of sun.

Step 28. Change to green sulky thread to attach grass. Adjust to shortest length available (Husqvarna Viking 936 Serger owners - see info display). Start serging on an anchor cloth. Serging on wrong side of quilt, cover stitch along marked line of grass.

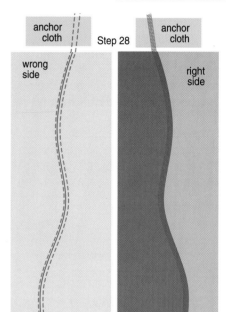

Step 29. Stuff sun with fiber fill. Stitch straight edges.

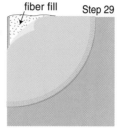

Step 30. Place mitered fences and horizontal fence rail on quilt top. Use straight stitch on sewing machine to tack in place.

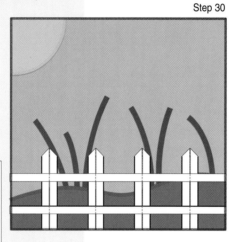

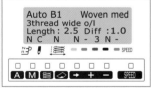

Auto B1   Woven med
3thread wide o/l
Length : 2.5 Diff :1.0
N C   N   N - 3 N -

Info display on a
Husqvarna Viking 936 Serger

Step 31. First make quilt sandwich by putting back of quilt on bottom, batting in middle and garden quilt on top. Set serger to 3 thread wide overlock using serger cone thread (Husqvarna Viking 936 Serger owners - see info display). Serge around edge of quilt. Width 5.0 To attach borders, leave serger on 3 thread overlock. Put borders on top and bottom first. Right sides together, sandwich quilt with border strips. Put border strip of batting on bottom layer. Serge cutting a blades width. Then serge outside layer together using blade as guide. Repeat process for sides. Add as many borders as desired.

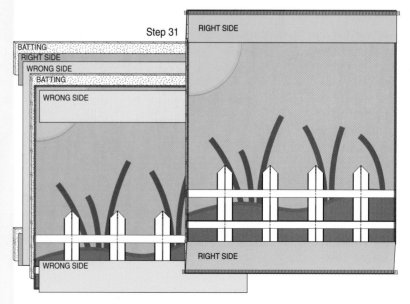

BINDING WITH SERGER

Cut binding strips 2 1/2" wide from selvage to selvage. Remove selvage edges.

Step 32. To connect strips end to end, put strips at a right angle, right sides together and sew at an angle as shown with sewing machine. Trim to 1/4" seam allowance and press open.

Step 33. Fold binding in half lengthwise, wrong sides together, and press.

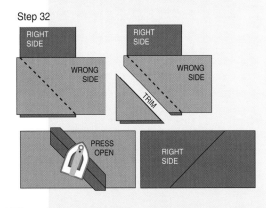

Step 32

Step 33

Step 34

Step 34. To save time, put Thread Fuse in lower looper if you don't want to hand sew binding to back of quilt. Leave info display on 3 thread overlock, width 7.0. Place binding on right side of quilt, making sure a seam does not fall on a corner; if it does, find a new place to start. Match edge of quilt to edge of binding. Finger pin (DO NOT USE PINS). Start serging about half of a cutting blade's width 4" from beginning of binding so end of binding can be slipped inside for a nice finish.

Step 35. Serge to 1/4" from corner of quilt edge. Lift presser foot. Turn hand wheel to lift needle to highest position. Pivot 90°. Drop presser foot. Serge 6" tail away from quilt.

Step 35

RIGHT SIDE OF QUILT

pivot point

1/4" from corner

Step 36. Turn your work and fold binding back. Binding edge and quilt edge should make a straight line when folded regardless of the angle of the quilt corner. This fold will start the miter on the corner.

Step 36

fold

Step 37. Place your finger on first fold and flip binding down to make the second fold even with binding; this will complete miter. Finger pin (DO NOT USE PINS) and start serging from the outside edge to 1/4" of next corner. Repeat steps #35 - #37 until you are around entire quilt.

Step 37

fold

Step 38

Step 38. Before you cut off end of binding, allow enough binding to be tucked inside at starting point. For a neat, finished look, fold 1/4" to inside of outer binding. Serge over opening.

fold

Step 39

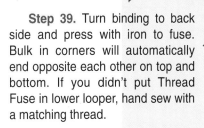

fold

back side of quilt

Step 39. Turn binding to back side and press with iron to fuse. Bulk in corners will automatically end opposite each other on top and bottom. If you didn't put Thread Fuse in lower looper, hand sew with a matching thread.

Hand stitch flowers in place on your garden quilt. Hope you have enjoyed learning how to use your serger.

Touch of Romance yardage

Finished Wall size 43" x 43"
four blocks

Queen size 92" x 108"
thirty blocks

PATTERN **290** COLOR **60**		

1/8 yard	2/3 yard	

PATTERN **291** COLOR **60**	
1/4 yard	1 1/3 yard

PATTERN **298** COLOR **49**	
1/8 yard	1 1/3 yard

PATTERN **299** COLOR **06**	
1/4 yard	1 1/3 yard

PATTERN **297** COLOR **66**	
1/4 yard	1 1/3 yard

PATTERN **296** COLOR **40**	
1/4 yard	1 1/3 yard
1/4 yard inside border	3/4 yard inside border

PATTERN **298** COLOR **60**	
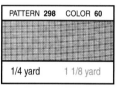	
1/4 yard	1 1/8 yard

PATTERN **293** COLOR **60**	
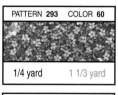	
1/4 yard	1 1/3 yard

PATTERN **292** COLOR **60**	

1/4 yard	1 1/3 yard
1 1/2 yards outside border & binding	3 1/2 yards outside border & binding
3 yards backing	9 yards backing

designed by
*Sharlene Jorgenson
& Andrea Poulimenos*
using the
Electric Quilt 5 software

pieced by
Phyllis Petersen

machine quilted by
Jean Johnson

Age of Innocence © designed by Sharlene Jorgenson for BENARTEX INC.

ABOUT THIS QUILT

Step 1. This romantic quilt was made with a variety of textures using light, medium, and dark prints from my new fabric collection, "Age of Innocence" by Benartex. The center square on point block is surrounded by eight flying geese units. The diagonal rows make this block unique. An eight pointed star is formed in the center of the quilt when four blocks are connected.

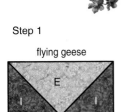

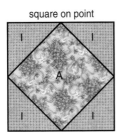

square on point

Step 1

flying geese

Step 2. Templates A, H, I, and E were used from the Peaky and Spike template set to make this quilt. Each block is 16" finished. This is a simple block when it is broken up into rows. Notice that there are arrows in the block that indicate the straight of grain of each piece. The straight of grain of shapes I and E changes depending on where they are used in the block. It is important to have the straight of grain on the outside edge of the block to keep it from getting distorted.

CUTTING INSTRUCTIONS FOR WALL QUILT

See page 4 to straighten fabric.

Step 3. Arrows on shapes in diagram indicate grain of fabric.

• Cut 1 strip 3 3/4" wide (3 different fabrics) for I's.

• Cut 3 strips 2 5/8" wide for I's used around outside edge of quilt block.

• Cut 1 strip 4 7/8" wide for E's used in corners of each quilt block.

• Cut 2 strips 3 1/2" wide (2 different fabrics) for E's used in center of block.

Step 4. Cut 1 strip 4 1/2" wide for template A used in center of block.

Cut 2 strips 3 3/8" wide for template H. Place strips on top of each other. Make sure edges are lined up before cutting. Remove selvage edge. See diagram for number of pieces to cut.

Step 2

16" finished

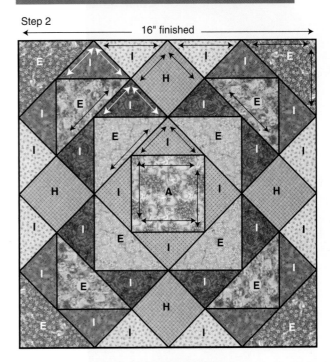

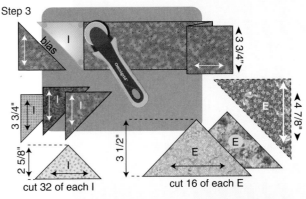

Step 3

cut 32 of each I

cut 16 of each E

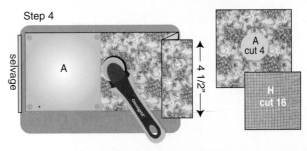

Step 4

A cut 4

H cut 16

Step 5

MAKING FLYING GEESE UNITS

Step 5a. Flying Geese units have two I sky background pieces and one E.

Step 5b

this seam
will not start
in crevice

Step 5b. Right sides together, place I sky on top of E. This seam will not start in crevice. There will be a couple stitches on the I. Do not back stitch at beginning or end of seam. Sew all seams with a scant 1/4" seam allowance (menu E stitch 1 on Husqvarna Viking Designers).

Step 5c

because seam does
not start in crevice
there is a tail

finger press
seam open

Step 5c. Finger press seam open. There is a tail as indicated by arrow because seam did not start in crevice.

Step 5d

anchor
cloth

do not
backstitch

seam ends
in crevice

Step 5d. Right sides together, add next I. Match points. Start sewing on anchor cloth so beginning stitches on patchwork will be more secure and won't pull apart as easily as first stitches sewn. This seam ends in crevice.

Step 5e

1/4"

E

Step 5e. Finger press seam open. Intersection should be 1/4" from edge.

Step 5f

1/4"

E

remove ears

Step 5f. Remove ears.

make 16

make 16

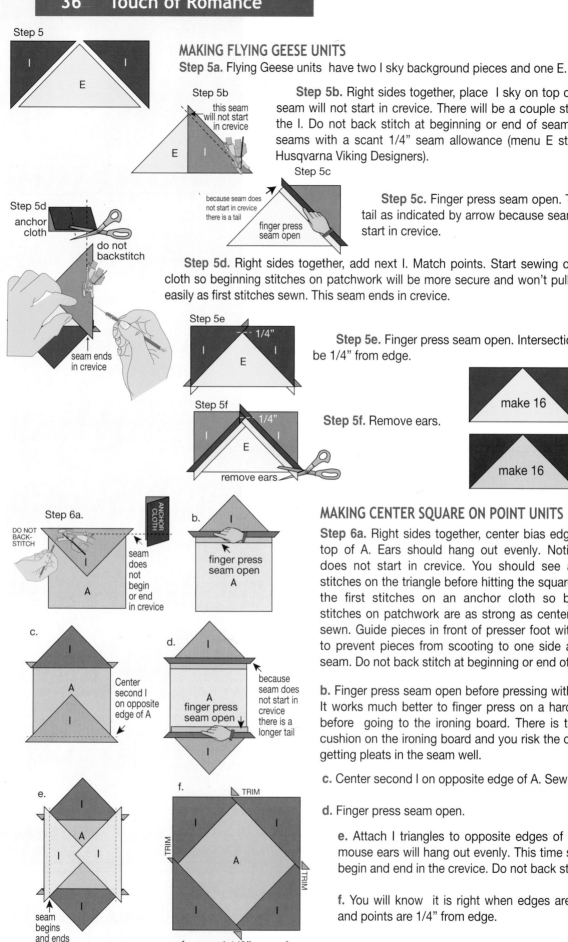

MAKING CENTER SQUARE ON POINT UNITS

Step 6a.

DO NOT
BACK-
STITCH

ANCHOR CLOTH

seam
does
not begin
or end
in crevice

A

Step 6a. Right sides together, center bias edge of I on top of A. Ears should hang out evenly. Notice seam does not start in crevice. You should see a couple stitches on the triangle before hitting the square. I make the first stitches on an anchor cloth so beginning stitches on patchwork are as strong as center stitches sewn. Guide pieces in front of presser foot with stiletto to prevent pieces from scooting to one side at end of seam. Do not back stitch at beginning or end of seam.

b.

I

finger press
seam open
A

b. Finger press seam open before pressing with an iron. It works much better to finger press on a hard surface before going to the ironing board. There is too much cushion on the ironing board and you risk the chance of getting pleats in the seam well.

c.

I

A

I

Center
second I
on opposite
edge of A

c. Center second I on opposite edge of A. Sew seam.

d.

I

A
finger press
seam open

I

because
seam does
not start in
crevice
there is a
longer tail

d. Finger press seam open.

e.

I

A

I   I

I

seam
begins
and ends
in crevice

e. Attach I triangles to opposite edges of unit. The mouse ears will hang out evenly. This time seam will begin and end in the crevice. Do not back stitch.

f.

TRIM

TRIM

I   I

A

TRIM

I   I

6 1/8"

f. You will know it is right when edges are straight and points are 1/4" from edge.

Make four of these units.

Step 7. Arrange units into diagonal rows.

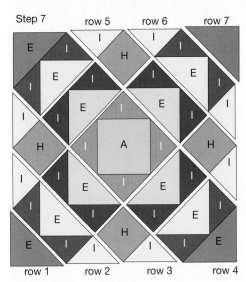

Step 7   row 5   row 6   row 7

row 1   row 2   row 3   row 4

Step 8. Connect I to H at both ends of rows 3 and 5 as shown below. The long edge of I was cut so it is on the straight of grain to keep the block from getting distorted. Right sides together, match corners. Do not back stitch at beginning or end of seam. This seam does not end in the crevice. Press seam open. Continue and add I's to both ends of Flying Geese units in rows 2 and 6.

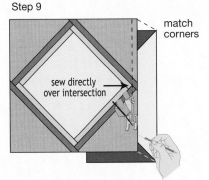

Step 8

I
H

this seam will not end in crevice

I   H

because seam does not start in crevice there is a tail

finger press seam open

Step 9. Continue connecting all units into diagonal rows. In diagram to the right, I show the center square on point unit on top of a flying geese unit so the intersection you want to sew over is visible. This gives you perfect points on the right side. Guide pieces in front of presser foot with stiletto to prevent pieces from scooting to one side at end of seam. Do not back stitch at beginning or end of seam. Connect all diagonal rows.

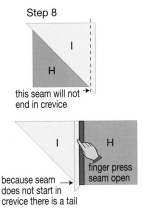

Step 9

match corners

sew directly over intersection

Step 10. Repeat steps 5-9 and make a total of four blocks. When four blocks are connected, a star is formed in the center (see page 34).

See page 7 to attach borders. See page 8 to make quilt sandwich.

The diagram below gives you quilting ideas.
See page 9 to attach binding.

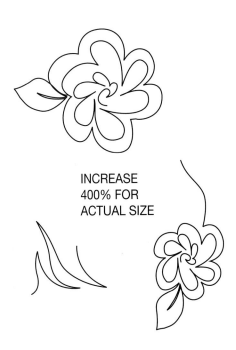

INCREASE
400% FOR
ACTUAL SIZE

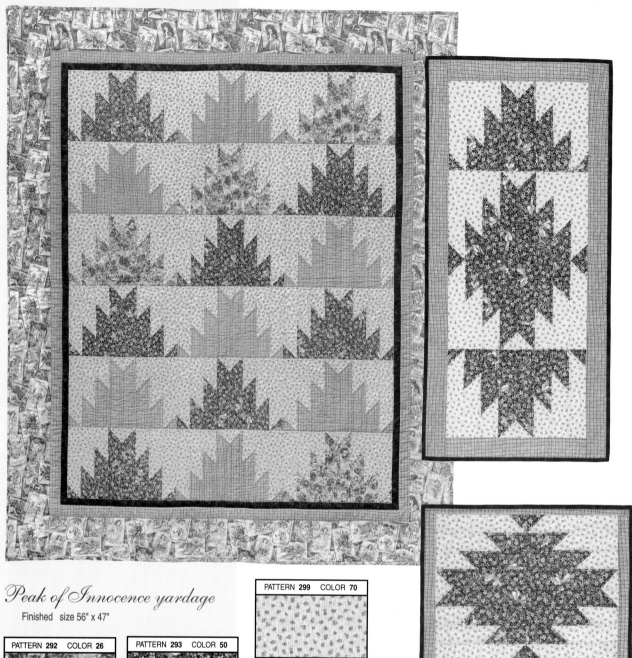

Peak of Innocence yardage

Finished   size 56" x 47"

PATTERN **292**   COLOR **26**
1/4 yard

PATTERN **293**   COLOR **50**
1/4 yard

PATTERN **298**   COLOR **02**
1/4 yard

PATTERN **298**   COLOR **50**
1/4 yard
1/2 yard inner   border

PATTERN **299**   COLOR **70**
1 3/4 yards

PATTERN **297**   COLOR **55**
1/4 yard inner border

PATTERN **300**   COLOR **50**

1 3/4 yards outside border & binding
4 yards backing

Age of Innocence
© designed by Sharlene Jorgenson for BENARTEX INC.

designed by
Brittany Tostenson
pieced by
Judy Blok
machine quilted by
Jean Johnson

Peak of Innocence

ABOUT THIS QUILT

This is a great quilt for beginners because there are very few points to match. Brittany first chose the post card print for the outside border which is from my new "Age of Innocence" collection by Benartex. Then she chose two pinks, two blues and one print with both pink and blue for the peaks. Make sure there is enough contrast between peaks and background so they don't mush together.

CUTTING INSTRUCTIONS

See page 4 to straighten the fabric.

Step 1. Cut strips 8 3/8" wide from both light and dark fabrics for the blocks. Remove selvage edges from end of strips. Next cut strips into 8 3/8" squares.

Cut 18 light squares and 18 dark squares from five different prints for the quilt on page 38.

Step 2. To keep directional prints all going the same direction in the quilt blocks, place squares right sides together before cutting them in half diagonally. Place ruler on blocks going from corner to corner and cut with rotary cutter.

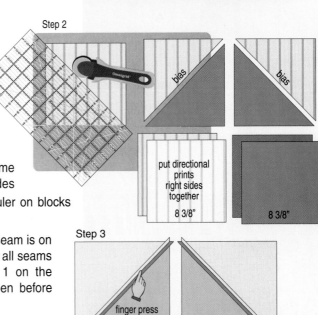

Step 2

bias   bias

put directional prints right sides together
8 3/8"   8 3/8"

Step 3. Sew light and dark triangles together. This seam is on the bias so be careful not to stretch it out of shape. Sew all seams with a scant 1/4" seam allowance (menu E stitch 1 on the Husqvarna Viking Designers). Finger press seams open before pressing with an iron. Remove ears.

You need two pieced triangle units for each block.

Step 3

finger press seam open

remove ears

Step 4. Place 6" x 12" ruler on top of triangles. Make sure straight edge of ruler matches 2" line on ruler. Cut four 2" strips from each block.

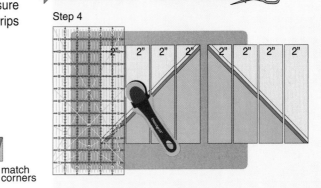

Step 4

2" 2" 2"   2" 2" 2" 2"

Step 5 Flip strips from step four 180° to form peaks.

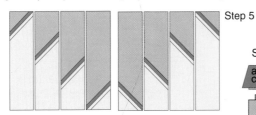

Step 5

Step 6. Place cut strips right sides together. Match corners. Put a pin at each end and one in the middle. Start sewing on an anchor cloth. Do not back stitch at beginning or end of seam. Use a stiletto to guide fabric in front of presser foot to prevent pieces from scooting to one side at the end of a seam.

Step 6

anchor cloth

match corners

match corners

Step 7. Each block should now measure 6 1/2" x 8".

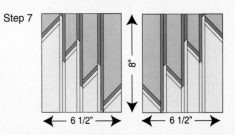

Step 7

8"

6 1/2"   6 1/2"

Step 8a

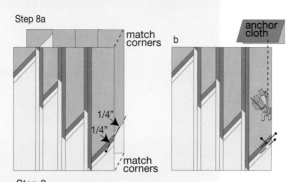

match corners

b

anchor cloth

1/4"
1/4"

match corners

Step 8a. To match point of middle seam, insert a pin 1/4" from edge on seam line through top and bottom. Leave this pin standing.

b. Insert a pin at angle shown on both sides of standing pin to hold intersection in place. Remove standing pin and sew seam.

Step 9

finger press seam open

8"

12 1/2"

Step 9. Finger press seam open before pressing with an iron. It is better to finger press seams open on a hard surface. Block measures 12 1/2" x 8". Make 18 blocks for quilt on page 38.

Step 10. Arrange blocks into rows and connect. Press seams open

Step 10

Step 11. There are many different ways to arrange the blocks.

Step 11

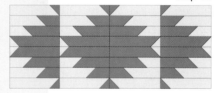

Step 12

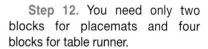

Step 12. You need only two blocks for placemats and four blocks for table runner.

Step 13

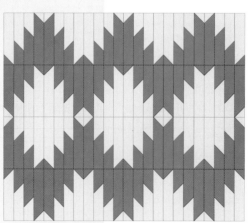

Step 13. Arrange units made in step seven as shown at left. Make equal amounts of each block for quilt layout at far left

Step 14

Step 14. The ric rac arrangement shown to the right is made with equal amounts of two blocks shown above. Have fun creating new ideas.

Step 15

Step 15. This quilt on page 38 has three borders. Cut strips for inside border 1 1/2" wide, middle border 2" wide and outside border 6" wide. Add border to top and bottom first, then to each side. Repeat to add all three borders.

Step 16

Step 16. See page 8 to make quilt sandwich. Using a Walking Foot, stitch 1/4" from edge of each piece of the peaks. The light background and outside border is filled with meandering using the Open Toe Stippling foot. Stitch 1/4" from edge of both small borders using the Walking foot. See page 14 for more quilting tips.

To attach binding see page 9.

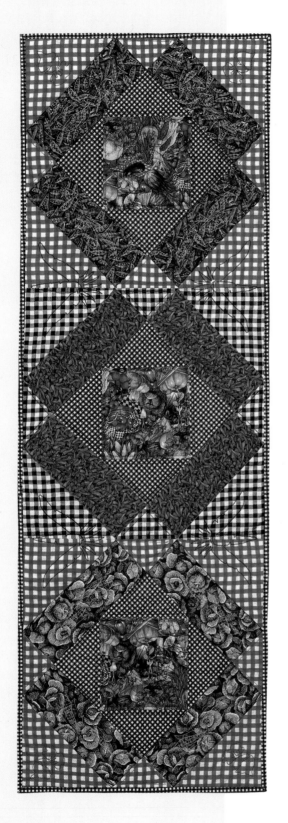

Grandma's Garden Yardage

14 1/2" x 41 1/2"	17 1/4" x 49 3/4"
1/4 yd.	1/4 yd.
1/4 yd.	1/4 yd.
1/2 yd.	1/2 yd.
1/4 yd.	1/4 yd.
1/8 yd.	1/8 yd.
1/8 yd.	1/8 yd.
1/8 yd.	1/8 yd.

designed. pieced,
and machine quilted by
Angela Scott

Grandma's Garden

ABOUT THIS TABLE RUNNER

The first fabric Angie chose was the main print which included all colors and vegetables she wanted. Then she added cabbage, peas, peppers and three different checked prints. These fun fabrics did not need a block with a lot of small pieces, instead she decided on a simple block that would show off the fabric.

CUTTING INSTRUCTIONS

Step 1. You are given cutting instructions for two table runner sizes. Follow black measurements for small size and red measurements for large size.

Cut corner triangles (B & E) in half diagonally as indicated in diagrams below. Short sides are on straight of grain and long side is on the bias.

Cut side triangles (D) in half diagonally in two directions as indicated in diagram below. Short sides are on bias and long side is on straight of grain. It's important to cut corner and side triangles so straight of grain ends up on outside edge of quilt.

SHOPPING LIST

Rotary Cutter
6" x 24" Omnigrid® Ruler
Glass Head Silk Pins 0.50mm
Large and small mat board
100% Merc. Cotton Sewing Thread
Stiletto
Warm & Natural cotton batting
Open toe stippling foot
Walking foot
Sulky 12 wt. thread

I INTERMEDIATE

■ = 14 1/2" x 41 1/2" tablerunner
■ = 17 1/4" x 49 3/4" tablerunner

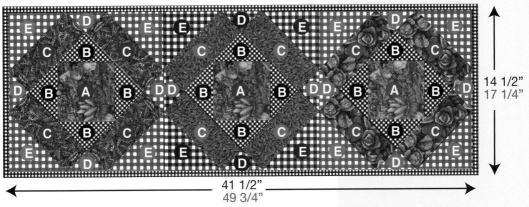

14 1/2"
17 1/4"

41 1/2"
49 3/4"

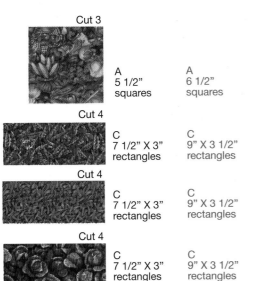

Cut 3

A
5 1/2"
squares

A
6 1/2"
squares

Cut 4

C
7 1/2" X 3"
rectangles

C
9" X 3 1/2"
rectangles

Cut 4

C
7 1/2" X 3"
rectangles

C
9" X 3 1/2"
rectangles

Cut 4

C
7 1/2" X 3"
rectangles

C
9" X 3 1/2"
rectangles

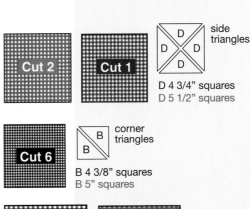

Cut 2

Cut 1

side triangles

D 4 3/4" squares
D 5 1/2" squares

Cut 6

corner triangles

B 4 3/8" squares
B 5" squares

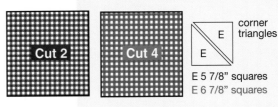

Cut 2

Cut 4

corner triangles

E 5 7/8" squares
E 6 7/8" squares

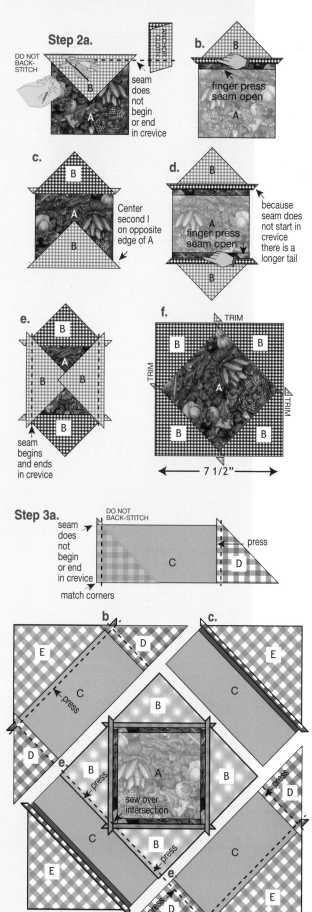

Step 2a.

DO NOT BACK-STITCH

seam does not begin or end in crevice

b. finger press seam open

c. Center second I on opposite edge of A

d. finger press seam open

because seam does not start in crevice there is a longer tail

e. seam begins and ends in crevice

f. TRIM TRIM TRIM

← 7 1/2" →

Step 3a.

DO NOT BACK-STITCH

seam does not begin or end in crevice

match corners

press

b. **c.**

press press

press press

sew over intersection

press

SEWING INSTRUCTIONS
Step 2

a. Sew all seams with a scant 1/4" seam allowance (menu E stitch 1 on Husqvarna Viking Designers). Start by making center square on point. Right sides together, center long (bias) edge of B triangle on top of A square. Ears should hang out evenly. Notice seam does not start in crevice. You should see a couple stitches on the triangle before hitting the square. I make the first stitches on an anchor cloth so beginning stitches on patchwork are as strong as center stitches sewn. Guide pieces in front of presser foot with stiletto to prevent pieces from scooting to one side at end of seam. Do not back stitch at beginning or end of seam.

b. Finger press seam open before pressing with an iron. It works much better to finger press on a hard surface before going to the ironing board. There is too much cushion on the ironing board and you risk the chance of getting pleats in seam wells.

c. Center second B on opposite edge of center A square and stitch.

d. Finger press seam open.

e. Attach B triangles to opposite edges of unit. The mouse ears will hang out evenly. This seam will begin and end in the crevice. Do not back stitch.

f. You will know it is right when edges are straight and points are 1/4" from edge. Make 3.

Step 3.

a. Right sides together, connect short end of D triangles to both ends of C rectangle. Match corners. This seam does not begin in the crevice. Press seam towards C rectangle.

b. Right sides together, center bias edge of E on top of C/D unit. Do not back stitch at beginning or end of seam. Press this seam open or to one side.

c. Center bias edge of E on top of C. Ears hang out evenly. This seam does not begin in the crevice. This seam can be pressed open or to one side.

d. Right sides together, place center square (made in step 2) on top of C/E unit so intersection you want to sew over is visible. Sew directly over intersection. Press seam out. Repeat on opposite side.

e. Right sides together, add corner units. Sew seam with square on point unit on top. Slide seams pressed in opposite directions together. Raised area of opposing seams helps to make a perfect match. This seam is pressed out (see arrows).

Repeat steps and make a total of three blocks for table runner. Notice the color placements change in each block.

To make quilt sandwich see page 8.

The continuous quilting designs on page 45 were used. See page 7 for instructions to transfer the quilting designs. Angie used Sulky 12 wt. cotton thread for quilting. See page 5 and 14 for machine quilting instructions. Using the Walking Foot stitch 1/4' from edge of each seam.

To attach binding see page 9.

ACTUAL SIZE CONTINUOUS LINE STENCILS
FOR MACHINE QUILTING

LAYOUT FOR STENCILS

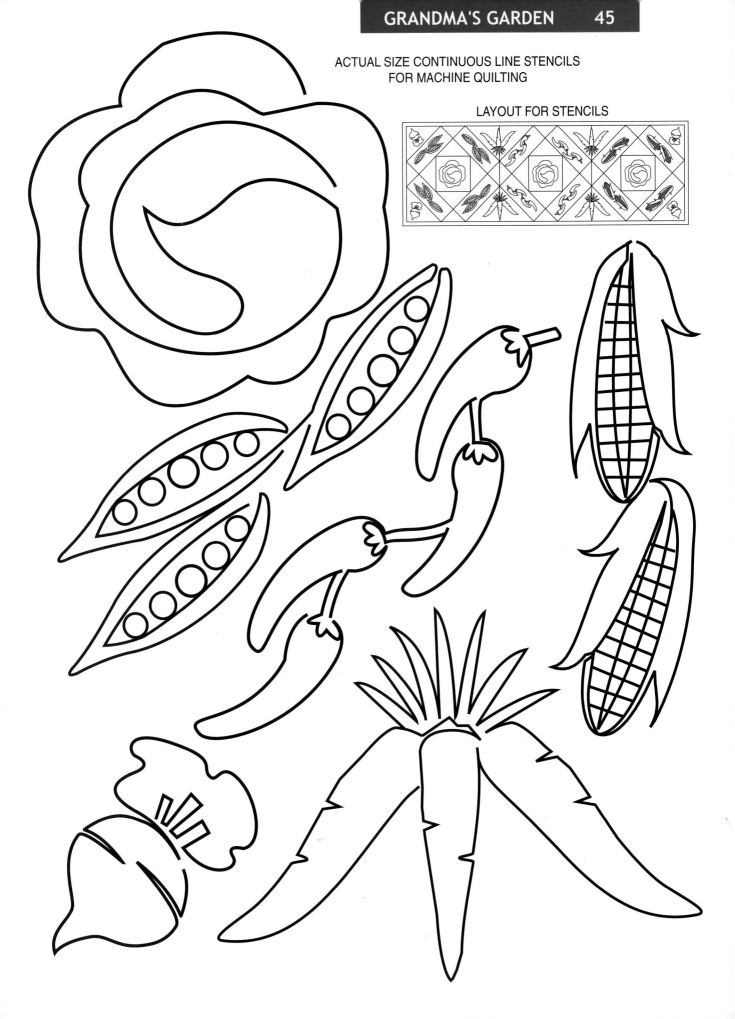

Trapunto Tulip yardage

Finished Wall size 57" x 57"
four blocks

King size 106" x 128 3/4"
twenty blocks

PATTERN 291	COLOR 07
1 3/4 yards	8 3/4 yards

PATTERN 293	COLOR 26
1/4 yard	1 1/4 yards

PATTERN 293	COLOR 50
1/2 yard	2 1/2 yards

PATTERN 297	COLOR 55
1/3 yard	1 2/3 yards
1/2 yard binding	1 yard binding

PATTERN 298	COLOR 50
1/3 yard	1 2/3 yards

PATTERN 290	COLOR 50
1/3 yard	1 2/3 yards

PATTERN 292	COLOR 26
1/4 yard	1 1/4 yards

PATTERN 297	COLOR 87
1/4 yard	1 1/4 yards
1/3 yard inside border	1 2/3 yards inside border

PATTERN 290	COLOR 26
1 5/8 yards outside border	8 1/8 yards outside border
3 1/2 yards backing	9 1/2 yards backing

designed by
Sharlene Jorgenson

pieced by
Marilyn Greene

machine quilted by
Sherry Rogers

Age of Innocence © designed by Sharlene Jorgenson for BENARTEX INC.

TRAPUNTO TULIP

ABOUT THIS QUILT

Step 1. This was a fun block to design because I was able to use nine prints from my "Age of Innocence" line by Benartex. The block is made up of two units made with Peaky & Spike templates. There is a tulip in each corner separated by a square on point. The dark blue print serves as a vase for the tulip and the blue plaid is a fence connecting the tulips. Doves in the center of each block make this a romantic tulip garden. The Trapunto Tulips show up so nicely on the cream Lily of the Valley background. The trapunto was stitched with a variegated Sulky 40 wt. rayon in a contrasting color to make it show up even more.

Step 1

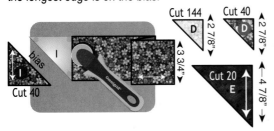

← 16" square finished →

CUTTING INSTRUCTIONS

See page 4 to straighten fabric.

These cutting instructions include blocks in corner of border.

Step 2. Templates A, B, C, D, E, H and I were used from Peaky & Spike. The triangles are all cut so the longest edge is on the bias.

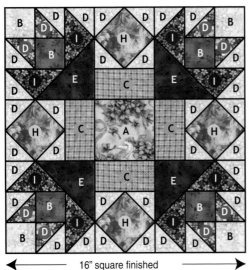

Cut 144 D   2 7/8"   3 3/4"
Cut 40 D   2 7/8"
Cut 20 E   4 7/8"
Cut 40 I

Step 3. Corner and side triangles were cut from the cream Lily of the Valley fabric.

■ Cut two 12 1/4" squares for corner triangles. Cut them in half diagonally. Short sides are on straight of grain and long side is bias.

■ Cut one 16 1/2" square for center block.

■ Cut one 24" square for side triangles. Cut them in half diagonally in two directions. Short sides are on bias and long side is on straight of grain. It's important to cut corner and side triangles so straight of grain ends up on outside edge of quilt. This also makes it easier to attach borders and prevent sagging.

NUMBER OF STRIPS AND PIECES TO CUT

E — Cut 20 E's, Cut two strips 4 7/8" wide

A — Cut 4 A's, Cut one strip 4 1/2" wide

I — Cut 40 I's, Cut three strips 3 3/4" wide

H — Cut 16 H's, Cut two strips 3 3/8" wide

D — Cut 40 D's, Cut three strips 2 7/8" wide

D — Cut 144 D's, Cut five strips 2 7/8" wide

C — Cut 16 C's, Cut one strip 4 1/2" wide

B — Cut 20 B's, Cut two strips 2 1/2" wide

B — Cut 20 B's, Cut two strips 2 1/2" wide

Step 2
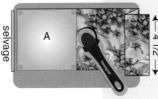

selvage   A ← 4 1/2"

A ← 4 1/2"   Cut 4

C ← 4 1/2"   Cut 16

H ← 3 3/8"   Cut 16

Step 3
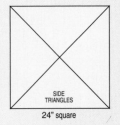

CORNER TRIANGLES   12 1/4" square

CENTER BLOCK   16 1/2" square

SIDE TRIANGLES   24" square

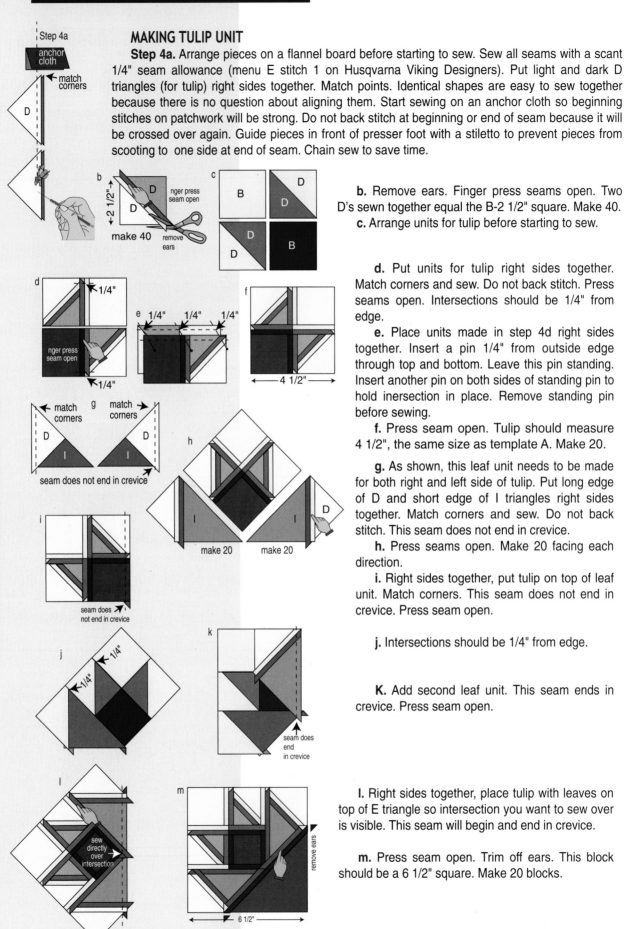

MAKING TULIP UNIT

Step 4a. Arrange pieces on a flannel board before starting to sew. Sew all seams with a scant 1/4" seam allowance (menu E stitch 1 on Husqvarna Viking Designers). Put light and dark D triangles (for tulip) right sides together. Match points. Identical shapes are easy to sew together because there is no question about aligning them. Start sewing on an anchor cloth so beginning stitches on patchwork will be strong. Do not back stitch at beginning or end of seam because it will be crossed over again. Guide pieces in front of presser foot with a stiletto to prevent pieces from scooting to one side at end of seam. Chain sew to save time.

b. Remove ears. Finger press seams open. Two D's sewn together equal the B-2 1/2" square. Make 40.

c. Arrange units for tulip before starting to sew.

d. Put units for tulip right sides together. Match corners and sew. Do not back stitch. Press seams open. Intersections should be 1/4" from edge.

e. Place units made in step 4d right sides together. Insert a pin 1/4" from outside edge through top and bottom. Leave this pin standing. Insert another pin on both sides of standing pin to hold inersection in place. Remove standing pin before sewing.

f. Press seam open. Tulip should measure 4 1/2", the same size as template A. Make 20.

g. As shown, this leaf unit needs to be made for both right and left side of tulip. Put long edge of D and short edge of I triangles right sides together. Match corners and sew. Do not back stitch. This seam does not end in crevice.

h. Press seams open. Make 20 facing each direction.

i. Right sides together, put tulip on top of leaf unit. Match corners. This seam does not end in crevice. Press seam open.

j. Intersections should be 1/4" from edge.

K. Add second leaf unit. This seam ends in crevice. Press seam open.

l. Right sides together, place tulip with leaves on top of E triangle so intersection you want to sew over is visible. This seam will begin and end in crevice.

m. Press seam open. Trim off ears. This block should be a 6 1/2" square. Make 20 blocks.

MAKING SQUARE ON POINT UNITS

Step 5a. Right sides together, center bias edge of D on top of H. Ears should hang out evenly. Notice seam does not start in crevice. You should see a couple stitches on the triangle before hitting the square. I make the first stitches on an anchor cloth so beginning stitches on patchwork are strong. Guide pieces in front of presser foot with stiletto. Do not back stitch at beginning or end of seam.

b. Finger press seam open before pressing with an iron. It works much better to finger press on a hard surface before going to the ironing board. There is too much cushion on the ironing board and you risk the chance of getting pleats in the seam well.

c. Center second D on opposite edge of H. Sew seam.

d. Finger press seam open before pressing with an iron.

e. Attach D triangles to opposite edges of unit. The mouse ears will hang out evenly. This time seam will begin and end in the crevice. Do not back stitch.

f. You will know it is right when edges are straight and points are 1/4" from edge.

Make sixteen of these units.

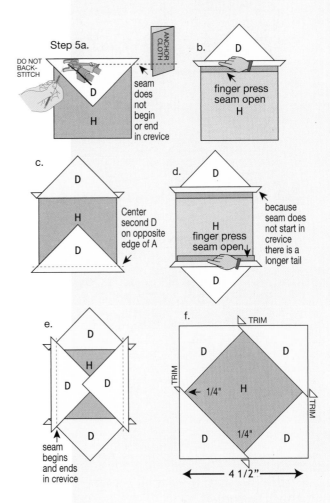

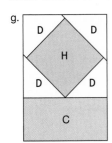

g. Place square on point unit on top of C rectangle so intersection you want to sew over is visible. Press seam towards the C rectangle.

Step 6. Arrange units into three rows. Place the A square in the center. Make sure tulips are turned in right direction. Place units right sides together. Insert a pin 1/4" from edge on the seam line. Leave this pin standing. Insert a pin on both sides of standing pin to hold intersection in place. Remove standing pin. Do not back stitch at beginning or end of seam. Press seam open. Continue until rows are connected. It should be a 16 1/2" square. Make four tulip blocks.

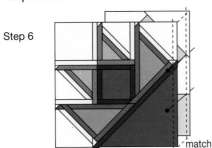

Step 6

match corners

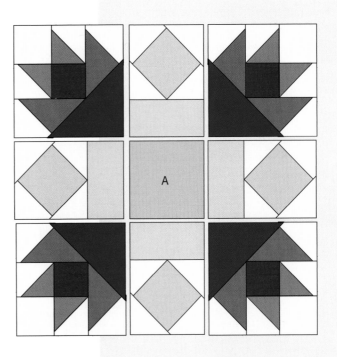

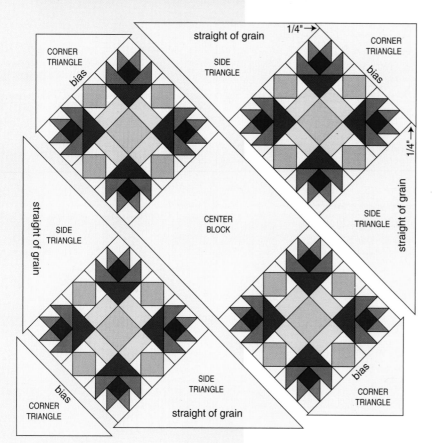

CONNECT UNITS INTO ROWS

Step 7. To finish quilt top, connect blocks into diagonal rows as shown. Corner and side triangles are also part of the diagonal rows. Right sides together, put tulip blocks on top so intersections you want to sew over are visible. Press seams towards the background (cream) fabric. The corner and side triangles are cut slightly oversized to allow for trimming quilt edges after assembly. Connect the rows. Do not trim 1/4" seam allowance off outside edge after triangles have been added; this is needed when adding inside border.

Attaching Borders

Step 8. Cut five strips 1 1/2" wide for inside border. Cut four strips 5 1/2" wide for outside border.

Put border strips right sides together and sew. Press seams open. Measure length of all four sides and take average measurement. Make borders to fit your measurement.

The next step is optional. Marilyn attached a piece of narrow border cut 1 1/2" wide on both ends before attaching to quilt. This makes a frame for corner tulips. This is a great idea if your fabric is slighty short for borders. Attach borders and press.

TRAPUNTO

Step 9. Enlarge the medalion tulip stencil (ST28-5) design 175% for center of the quilt. Enlarge single tulip sencil (ST28-6) 175% for side triangles. Use the single tulip stencil ST28-6 in actual size for corner triangles. Trace continuous line quilting designs with water soluble pen onto Golden Thread quilting paper. For multiple copies, cut several sheets to desired size. Pin or staple together with traced design on top. Stitch with large unthreaded needle following the design to needle punch through all layers. Pin just one layer to project.

Pin a piece (large enough to cover whole design) of Warm & Natural polyester batting to wrong side of quilt top under trapunto design. Pin to hold in place.

Golden Threads Quilting Paper

BATTING

Step 10. Thread upper machine needle with water-soluble thread. Use cotton thread in bobbin. Attach open toe stippling foot to machine and disengage the feed dogs. Set Husqvarna Viking designers on V menu (special stitches) stitch 1. Now you can move your machine in any direction. The length of your stitches is determined by how fast you move your fabric and the speed you run your machine.

Put your quilt under needle and draw bottom thread up through fabric. Holding both threads, take a few stitches in one place. Cut loose threads. Free motion with water soluble thread on lines indicated in the diagram.

Start sewing at a slow speed and move the quilt as you sew. You will feel tension between the quilt and needle. If you move the quilt too fast, you may break a needle. If you move it too slow your stitches may be too small. Now increase the speed of your machine and begin to move quilt at a steady, even pace. Stop stitching where lines intersect. Avoid stopping on curves because it is hard to get started with exactly the same stitch length.

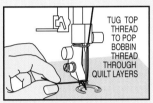

TUG TOP THREAD TO POP BOBBIN THREAD THROUGH QUILT LAYERS

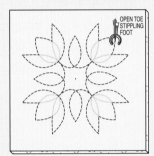

OPEN TOE STIPPLING FOOT

Step 11. Turn quilt to wrong side. Use a blunt scissor to remove batting from areas you don't want to be stuffed. Cut as close as possible to stitching.

Repeat and do trapunto in all corner and side triangles.

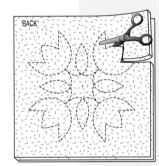

BACK

BACK

Step 12. Now you are ready to finish your quilting. See page 8 to make quilt sandwich. Put Warm & Natural cotton batting in middle layer. Cut backing and batting so that it extends 2 -3 beyond quilt top.

Sherry used variegated 40 wt. rayon to free motion quilt all lines of the design. She filled the background around the tulips with meandering. The tulip border stencil ST28-7B was used in the border. She enlarged the tulip design again to quilt over the patchwork.

Step 13. See page 9 for binding instructions.

designed, pieced, and
machine quilted by

Lois K. Fletcher

Sno 'n Love Table Runner Yardage

Finished size 18 1/2" x 46 1/2"

Five plaids
for Flying Geese
1/4 yd. each

White for Snow,
Snowpeople, and backing
1 1/3 yd.

Background plaid
3/4 yd.

Scarves and letters
8" x 8"

Tree top – 3" x 5"

Noses – 1 1/2" x 3"

Tree middle – 4" x 7"

Inner border
1/8 yd.

Tree bottom – 5" x 7"

Middle border and binding
1/2 yd.

Tree trunk – 1 1/2" x 1 1/2"

Sno 'n Love

FUSIBLE WEB APPLIQUÉ INSTRUCTIONS

Step 1. Trace each appliqué shape, on pages 56 and 57, separately on smooth side of Trans Web or your favorite iron-on adhesive. Long dashed lines indicate where shapes overlap. Be sure to allow space between shapes so each can be cut loosely around tracing lines. Mark template number on each piece because you will be assembling appliqué shapes in numerical order.

Note: In this pattern trace two sets of pieces 1 - 9. One set should be traced in reverse because the snowpeople are facing opposite directions on both ends of tablerunner. This can be done one of two ways. First, you can copy template pieces on a copy machine that has mirror-image capability. Second, you can trace the design onto a piece of plain paper, then place paper wrong side up over a light source such as a window or light box. Trace design though paper onto back side. Use this side as your pattern.

Step 2. Cut each paper shape approximately 1/4" from your drawing line.

Step 3. Fuse appliqué shapes to wrong side of appropriate fabrics. (Hint: When fusing scarves and "winter" letters, turn pieces at a 45° angle to the weave of the plaid.)

Cut out each of the appliqué pieces following drawing line on paper side of fusible web. After pieces have been fused to wrong side of fabric and cut to shape, they will be facing the same direction as seen in quilt photo.

SUPPLIES

SP1 Peaky and Spike templates
Fabric grips
Rotary cutter
Mat board
6" x 24" Omnigrid® ruler
Glass Head Silk Pins 0.05 mm
Stiletto
Marking pencil
20 black 1/8"-diameter buttons
Black Sulky® 12 wt. thread
Open Toe Foot
Warm & Natural® cotton batting
Appliqué Pressing Sheet
Trans Web Stabilizer
Tear Away Light Stabilizer by America Sews

B BEGINNER

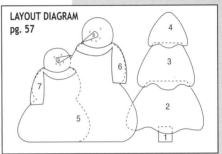

LAYOUT DIAGRAM
pg. 57

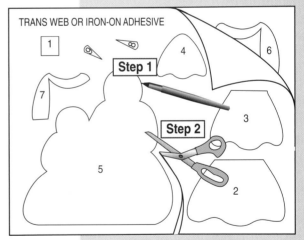

TRANS WEB OR IRON-ON ADHESIVE

Step 1

Step 2

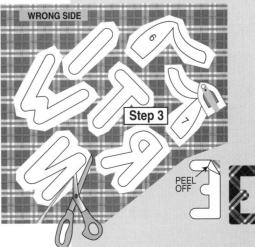

WRONG SIDE

Step 3

PEEL OFF

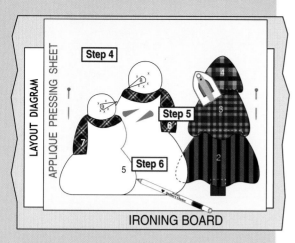

Step 4. To achieve greater accuracy in aligning the fusible shapes, you will make an appliqué unit first. Do this by placing the layout diagram (the reverse image of the template pieces being used) on the ironing board. Note: Since a reverse image has been created in Step 1, you have a layout diagram for both snowpeople blocks.

Lay appliqué pressing sheet over placement diagram and pin both to ironing-board cover. This prevents layout from shifting while arranging appliqué pieces.

Step 5. In numerical order, place appliqué pieces on pressing sheet over placement diagram. Each time a piece is added, press with iron. After all pieces have been fused together, let appliqué unit cool. Remove unit from pressing sheet.

Step 6. Using a fine pencil, lightly trace detail line that separates snowpeople (shown as a dotted line on the appliqué template). If detail line is difficult to see through fabric, place it over a light box. This will be the stitching line.

CUTTING INSTRUCTIONS

Step 7. To straighten fabric, see page 4. From background plaid, cut one strip 7 3/4" x 36 1/2" wide for background.

From white fabric, cut 1 strip 1 1/2" wide.

From burgundy fabric, cut 3 strips 3/4" wide.

From navy blue fabric, cut 3 strips, each 1 1/4" wide.

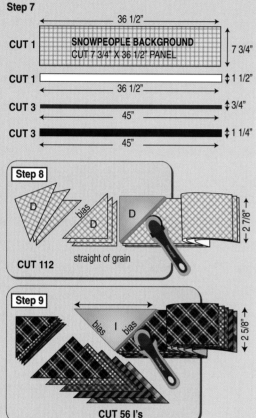

Step 8. Cut 4 strips from background plaid, 2 7/8" wide. Place strips on top of each other. Make sure edges are in line. Place template D on top of strips as shown so bias is on longest edge. Cut 112 D triangles.

Step 9. From five blue plaid fat quarters, cut 2 strips 2 5/8" wide. Place strips on top of each other. Make sure edges are in line. Place template I on top of strips as shown so bias is on shortest edge. With the I template cut 56 triangles.

PREPARATION OF TABLE RUNNER

Step 10. With a scant 1/4" seam allowance, sew a 1 3/4" x 36 1/2" white strip (snow) to one long side of a 7 3/4" x 36 1/2" background rectangle. Press seam towards snow.

Step 11. Place snowpeople appliqué units on background, aligning bottom of snowpeople with seam line; fuse in place.

Step 12. Arrange WINTER letters in an even horizontal line or skew them slightly as shown. After letters are arranged, fuse to background block.

Step 13. You may want to put a tear away light stabilizer under areas to be appliqued. Appliqué with a blanket stitch around all shapes. When done, press. Place the 1 1/4" line of ruler over background seam line and trim excess fabric from bottom. Trim block to 8 1/2" high. Design is now centered on a panel 8 1/2" x 36 1/2".

Step 14. With a scant 1/4" seam allowance, sew the 3/4" x 36 1/2" burgundy inner border strips to top and bottom of tablerunner. Trim seams to 1/8" and press toward border. Sew 3/4" x 9" strips to each side of table runner. Trim seams to 1/8" and press toward border. This should measure 36 3/4" x 9 1/4".

Step 15. With a scant 1/4" seam allowance, sew the 1 1/4" x 37" navy blue inner border strips to top and bottom of table runner. Press seams toward border. Sew 1 1/4" x 10 1/2" inner border strips to each side of table runner. Press seams toward border. This should measure 38 1/2" x 10 3/4".

CONSTRUCTING FLYING GEESE BORDERS

Step 16. Flying Geese have two D background pieces and one blue plaid I. Place one background-plaid D triangle on one blue-plaid I triangle, matching one corner as indicated by arrow. Beginning in this corner, stitch triangles together. This seam does not start in the crevice. There will be a couple stitches on the D triangle. Do not backstitch at beginning or end of seam. Chain sew 56 of these units. Guide pieces in front of presser foot with stiletto to prevent pieces from scooting to one side at end of seam. Finger press seams open.

Step 17. Right sides together, add next D. Match points. Start sewing on an anchor cloth so beginning stitches will be more secure and won't pull apart as easily as first stitches sewn. Do not back stitch at beginning or end of seam. This seam will end in crevice.

Finger press seam open. Intersection should be 1/4" from edge.

Remove ears.

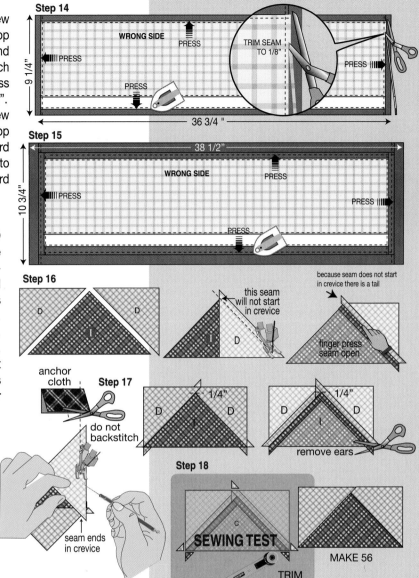

Step 18. The sewn unit should equal template C. If not, correct your seam allowance before continuing. Make 56.

Step 19. To make top and bottom borders, sew 19 Flying Geese units together into one long strip with all points facing the same direction. Make 2. Press seams away from points. This should measure 38 1/2" x 4 1/2".

Step 20. Find midpoint of table runner center and the Flying Geese border by folding in half and marking with a straight pin. With midpoints and ends aligned and borders arranged as shown, stitch borders to top and bottom edges of table runner center. Press seams toward inner borders.

Step 21. To make side borders, sew 7 Flying Geese units together into one long strip as in step 19. Make 2. Press seams away from points. This should measure 14 1/2" x 4 1/2".

Sew remaining Flying Geese units into pairs. Sew one of these pairs to one end of each long strip, orienting them as shown. Press seam toward long strip. This should measure 18 1/2 x 4 1/2".

Find midpoint of table runner sides and side-border strips. Mark with a straight pin. With midpoints and ends aligned and borders arranged as shown, stitch the borders to the side edges of the table runner. Press seams toward the inner borders.

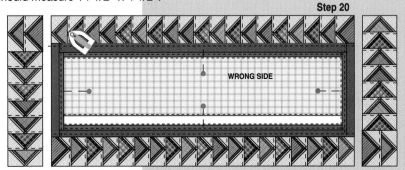

FINISHING TOUCHES

Make a quilt sandwich by layering batting between backing and table runner. Thin cotton is preferred. Baste with safety pins or basting spray.

Use Sulky invisible thread in top needle and thread to match quilt back in bobbin. Starting in the center of the table runner, stitch around each appliqué shape. Stipple quilt around the appliqués in the background fabric. Stitch in the ditch around both inner borders and the Flying Geese units.

See page 9 for instructions to bind the table runner. Sew the 20 black, 1/8"-diameter buttons on the table runner as indicated by x's on the templates and layout diagram on page 57.

ACTUAL SIZE
LETTER
TEMPLATES

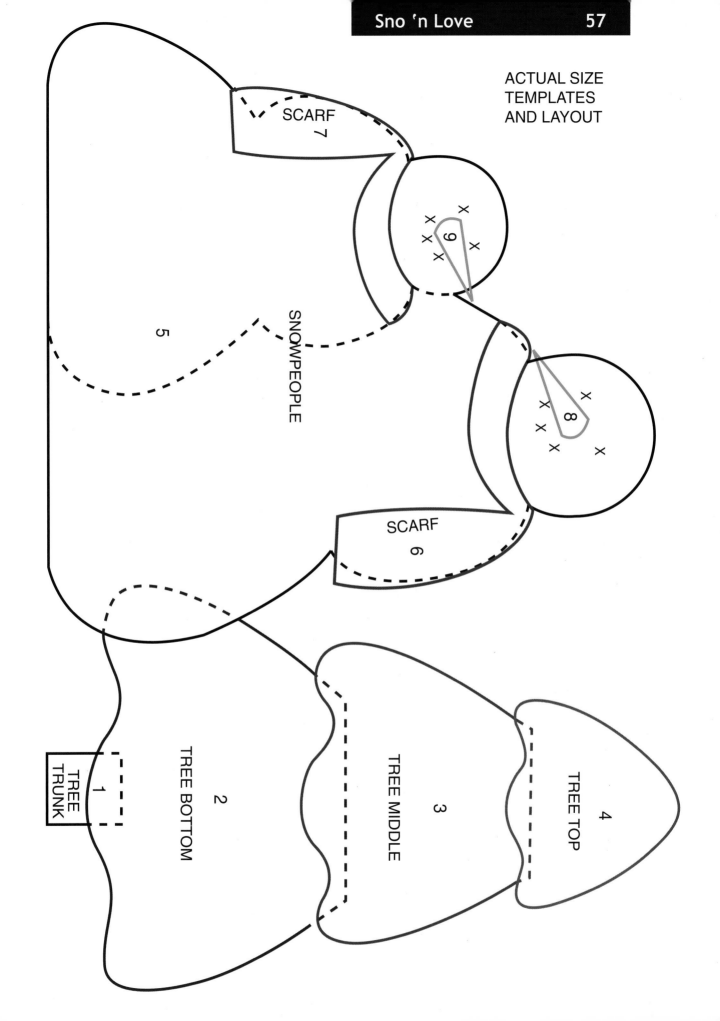

ACTUAL SIZE
TEMPLATES
AND LAYOUT

SCARF
7

9

5

SNOWPEOPLE

8

SCARF
6

TREE
TRUNK
1

2
TREE BOTTOM

3
TREE MIDDLE

4
TREE TOP

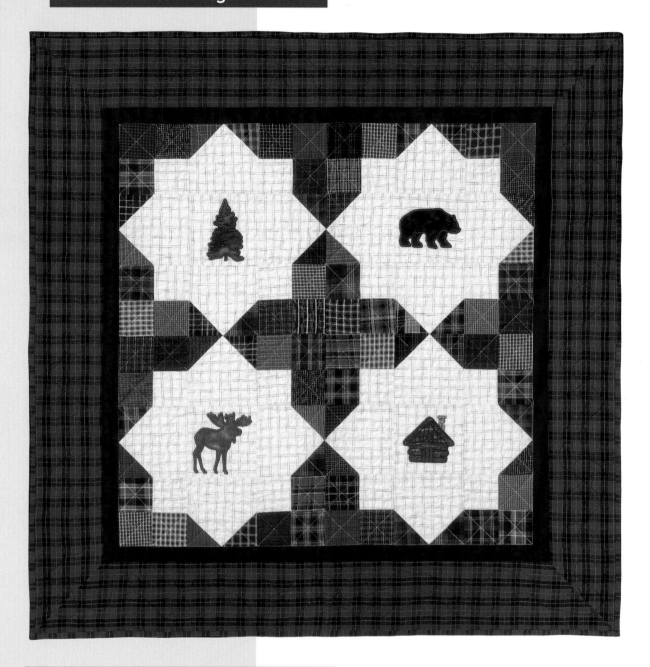

Winter Lodge Yardage
finished size 33 1/2" x 33 1/2"

3/4 yd.

20 fat eighths
or scraps

1/4 yd. inside border

3/4 yd. outside border
and binding

7/8 yd. backing

Embroidery designs by
Lindee Goodall of Cactus Punch

designed, pieced, and
machine quilted by
Sharlene Jorgenson

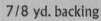

Winter Lodge

About This Quilt

I used twenty different plaids and stripes from my stash for the scrappy look in this quilt. The more scraps used, the better it will look. Select a palette to keep it from getting confused and haphazard. I limited the colors to reds, blues, greens and browns. The light cream plaid is a perfect contrasting background for the Northwoods appliques. Crosshatching was quilted with the Walking Foot and I meandered around the appliques. It needed the narrow black inside border to separate the plaids in the quilt from the outside border. A continuous line star design was quilted in the outside border. There is a Northwoods Applique by Cactus Punch in the center of each block.

SUPPLIES

B BEGINNER

SP1 Peaky & Spike templates
Fabric grips
Rotary cutter
Large and small mat board
6" x 24" Omnigrid® ruler
Glass Head Silk Pins 0.05 mm
Stiletto
Sulky® rayon 40 wt. thread
Sulky® Totally Stable
Open Toe Foot
Walking Foot
Warm & Natural® cotton batting
NATO1 Nature 1 Northwoods Appliques *by Cactus Punch*
Golden Threads Quilting Paper
Steam-A-Seam® Fusible Web
ST-S Millennium Star stencil
Card stock paper
Mini Clover Iron

Cutting Instructions

Step 1. You only need to use two shapes (template A and B) from Peaky & Spike.

Cut two strips 4 1/2" wide from cream background.

Cut one strip 2 1/2" wide from cream background.

Place strips the same width on top of each other making sure edges are in line. Bifold strips on a small mat board so it is easier to turn your work as you cut around the template. Place A template on top of 4 1/2" strips cutting pieces as you go. Cut 16 A's.

Place B template on 2 1/2" strip. Cut 16 cream B's.

Cut four 8" x 10" pieces from cream fabric for appliques.

If you want to machine applique the center of each block follow steps 6-11 on page 61. Use template A to fussy cut the appliques.

Step 2. Place up to six scraps on top of each other on a small mat board. Don't worry if the plaids and stripes are slightly off grain. When cutting around the template make first cut going backwards off the fabric. Then, starting in the same place, continue to cut away from yourself.

If you are using a lot of each fabric, cut it into 2 1/2" strips. Then cut B's from strips. You need a total of 80 B's.

Arrange pieces for each block on a flannel board to get the colors evenly distributed. Some squares are folded to see the design.

Step 1

A

4 1/2"

A
cut 16

B
cut 16

fussy cut

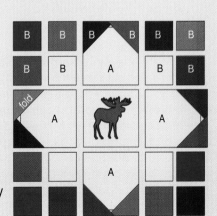

Step 2

B

B
cut 80

Step 4

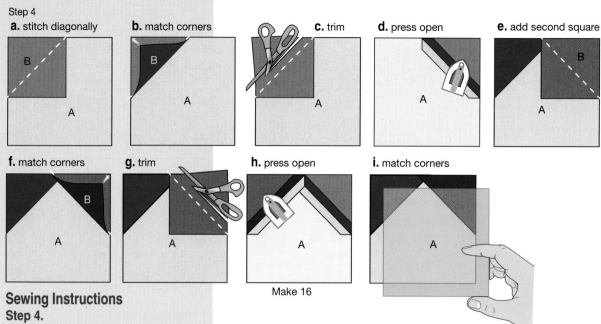

a. stitch diagonally **b.** match corners **c.** trim **d.** press open **e.** add second square

f. match corners **g.** trim **h.** press open **i.** match corners

Make 16

Sewing Instructions

Step 4.

a. Place a small 1" x 6" ruler from corner to corner on the wrong side of B piece. Use a Chalk-O-Liner or chalk pencil to make a diagonal line on the wrong side of each B piece.

Right sides together, place B on top of A. With needle in center needle position stitch diagonally. If your machine wants to eat the fabric at the beginning, it is helpful to start sewing on an anchor cloth. Do not back stitch at beginning or end of the seam.

b. Fold B along seam line and match corners. Redo your seam if if you don't have a nice square corner.

c. Trim to 1/4" seam allowance.

d. Finger press seam open then press with an iron.

e. Right sides together place second square on top of unit. Sew diagonal seam.

f. Fold corner back to see if you have a good match.

g. If you have a good match in the corner, trim seam allowance to 1/4".

h. Finger press seam open, then press with an iron. Intersection will be 1/4" from the edge.

i. You can check your sewing by placing template A on top of unit and trim off any excess. If the unit is too small, you need to make corrections or start another one.

Step 5

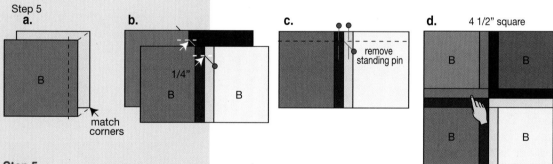

a. **b.** 1/4" **c.** remove standing pin **d.** 4 1/2" square

match corners

Step 5

a. Place a dark and light B square right sides together. Match corners. Start sewing on an anchor cloth so beginning stitches will be as strong as middle stitches sewn. Sew all seams with a scant 1/4" seam allowance (menu E stitch 1 on Designers). Do not backstitch at either end of seam. Repeat and sew two dark B's together.

b. Finger press seam open before pressing with an iron. Place two rows of B's right sides together. Insert a pin 1/4" from outside edge on seam line through top and bottom. Leave this pin standing.

c. On both sides of standing pin, insert another pin to hold intersection in place. Remove standing pin. Do not back stitch at either end of seam.

d. Finger press seam open, then press with an iron. Place template A on top of unit to check your sewing. Each unit should be a 4 1/2" square. Make four for each block.

MAKING APPLIQUE PATTERN

Step 6. Use masking tape to attach a sheet of card stock (a 4" x 6" card works well) to bottom of embroidery hoop. Use quilters mylar if you are going to use the design many times. Slide hoop on embroidery arm. Select an applique design. Put applique R foot on machine. With a large unthreaded used needle, stitch only the outline of applique. This outlline is usually the first color on a single piece applique design, refer to color sequence information to verify. Touch START/STOP to begin embroidery. Remove hoop from machine and label template within the needle perforations as shown in step 6. If you forget feel the needle holes. The smooth side of pattern is right side and the rough side is wrong side. Indicate right and wrong side on your pattern. Remove card stock from hoop.

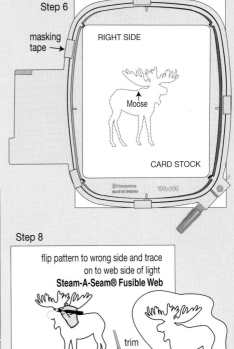

Step 7. Carefully cut out pattern precisely following perforations.

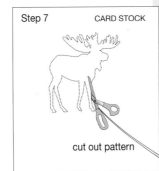

Step 8. Turn card stock pattern to wrong side and trace to web side of Steam-A-Seam® Fusible Web. Peel off paper liner. Use light color pencil when working on dark fabric.

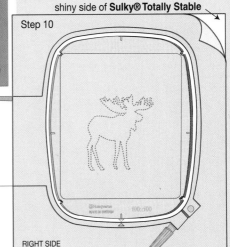

Step 9. Stick Steam-A-Seam® to wrong side of fabric. Cut your fabric and Steam-A-Seam® together along traced line. Once again, precision cutting is a must for a perfect end result.

APPLIQUE

Step 10. Touch the minus and go back to first color. Thread embroidery needle with Sulky rayon and put bobbin thread in bobbin.

Cut a piece of Sulky® Totally Stable large enough to be hooped. Press shiny side of Totally Stable to wrong side of 8" x 10" fabric to be appliqued on. Hoop fabric and Totally Stable. Slide hoop onto the embroidery arm.

Touch START/STOP to begin embroidery. Machine will stop after it has sewn the outline stitch. You may remove hoop from machine but, **do not remove fabric from hoop.**

Step 11. Place applique inside outline stitch. Carefully press in place with a mini clover iron for 10-15 seconds while still in hoop. Slow down the machine speed so if you see a problem, you can correct it. Continue sewing. The second time around the machine will zig zag to hold applique in place. Lindee likes to stop the machine after these tack down stitches have sewn to inspect the applique. If any fabric is extending beyond the stitching, she then carefully trims off the excess. Reset the speed back to high and finish the design as usual.

Repeat these applique steps for remaining appliques.

Connecting Rows

Step 12. Arrange units into rows as shown for each block. Start with top row. Put two units right sides together. Insert a pin 1/4" from the edge on the seam line through the top and bottom unit. Leave this pin standing. Insert another pin on both sides of standing pin. Remove standing pin and sew seam with scant 1/4" seam allowance. Press seam open.

Continue connecting units into rows. Connect the rows. Make four 12 1/2" blocks. Connect the blocks.

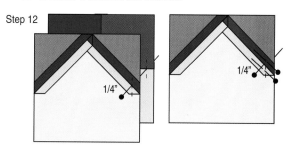

Step 13. Cut four strips 1 1/2" wide for inner border. Cut four strips 4 1/4" wide for outer border. Attach inner border to top and bottom. Press seams open. Add inner borders to sides. Press seams open. Repeat and add outer borders.

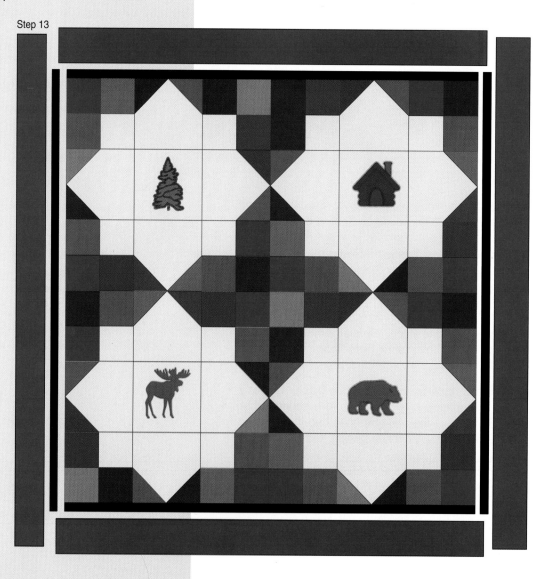

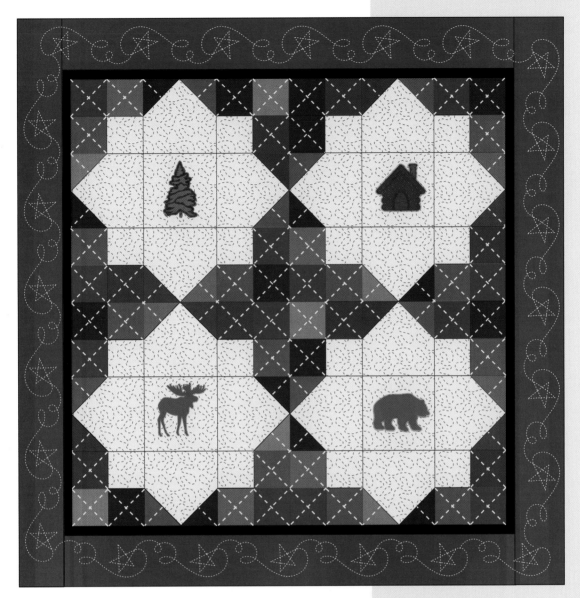

Step 14. See page 8 to make quilt sandwich. I used Warm & Natural cotton batting. The crosshatching was quilted with a Walking Foot. Meandering around the appliques was done with an open toe stippling foot. The continuous line Millenium Star stencil was used in the border.

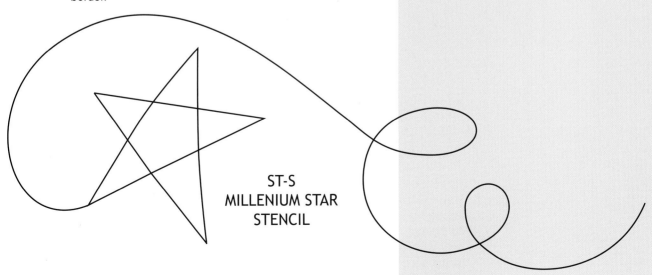

ST-S
MILLENIUM STAR
STENCIL

Beginning with Finishing Touches

SHOPPING LIST
Golden Thread Paper
Quilting thread
Open-Toe Stippling Foot
Quilting needle
Warm & Natural® cotton batting
Earthline Flowers by Julie Mullin
Permanent marking pencil
Free-Motion Guide Grip
Walking Foot

ABOUT NO MARKING METHOD

Julie Mullin looks at a quilt from a different perspective. She chooses the continuous quilting design before picking the patchwork design. Angie had already made this quilt before Julie saw it so in this case quilting designs were picked last.

Free motion quilting works best for continuous line designs, stippling, outlining flowers, and feathered designs. This No-Marking Method of machine quilting eliminates the need for marking your quilt top. This method will save you the time it takes to mark and remove the marks from quilt top, while eliminating the worry of leaving permanent marks on your fabric. Creating your own tear-away stencils will guarantee always having the right size and quantity of repeats you need to complete your project. Your original remains intact for use on other projects.

Julie says you don't have to invest a lot in your work space. She put a table that she purchased at a garage sale up against the wall to support the quilt so it doesn't fall off the edge and drag while quilting.

Step 1. Julie chose spring flowers to compliment the flowers in the "Age of Innocence" fabric. The Pansy at each intersection fills the space well and the continuous leaf design is a perfect connector between the Pansies. The largest area has a Pansy surrounded by a circle of leaves.

Step 1

Step 2

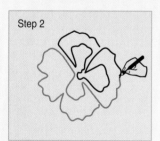

Step 2. Trace continuous line quilting design onto Golden Thread Quilting Paper with a permanent marker.

Step 3

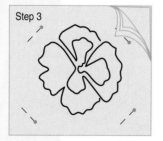

Step 3. For multiple copies when using the same design in several blocks, stack layers (up to 15) of paper together placing traced design on top. Pin together.

Step 4

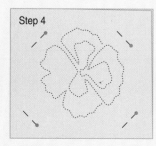

Step 4. Prepare machine for free motion quilting. Before attaching Open Toe Stippling Foot, take standard ankle and presser foot off the machine. Place Open Toe Stippling Foot on the presser bar. Screw in place with the accessory thumb screw. Lower the feed teeth and set presser foot pressure to the darning position. (For Designer I, Designer II, or Quilt Designer, select the V menu, touch free motion straight stitch V1). Stitch with large unthreaded needle following the design to needle punch through all layers.

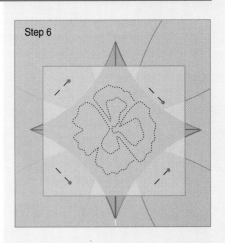

Step 6

Step 5. See page 8 to make quilt sandwich by hand basting. There are other methods of basting the quilt sandwich together. Pin basting or basting on a long arm machine is fast. It is easier to machine quilt with cotton batting because it clings to the fabric.

Step 6. Don't use top layer of paper if it has a pencil mark that would get embedded in the quilt. Pin just one layer of needle punched paper to quilt. Because the paper is transparent it is easy to position the design over the quilt.

Step 7. Thread machine with a thread that's one shade darker than fabric and cotton thread to match back in bobbin. Julie uses a dove gray or darker gray on bottom. Switch needles depending on size of thread you use. The thicker the thread the larger the eye of the needle. Angie and Shar like to use a top stitching needle when quilting with 12 wt. Sulky thread.

Keep feed dogs in lowered position. We suggest you practice on scraps before starting on a quilt top. It is also a good idea to practice if you haven't done it for a while.

Start quilting in center of quilt. Put your quilt under needle and draw bottom thread up through fabric. Holding both threads, take a few stitches in one place. Cut threads.

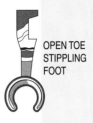

OPEN TOE STIPPLING FOOT

TUG TOP THREAD TO POP BOBBIN THREAD THROUGH QUILT LAYERS

Step 8. Make sure your quilt is well supported and free of stress. Start sewing at a slow speed and move the quilt as you sew. You will feel tension between the quilt and needle. If you move the quilt too fast, you may break a needle. If you move it too slow your stitches may be too small. Now increase the speed of your machine and begin to move quilt at a steady, even pace.

Because there is so much happening at one time, it's easy to get tense. Remember to breathe and relax when machine quilting. After all, this is fun! Listening to your favorite music is relaxing.

Look where you're going, not at needle. If you sew too slowly, stitches will be long and if you sew too fast there will be too many stitches per inch. Practice improves your skills. Have fun with it. Just like hand quilting,

Step 9. Angie likes to use the Free Motion Guide Grip to move the quilt while quilting and Julie likes to just grab the quilt to control it. Either way you can freely move it forward, backward and from side to side. Move quilt or fabric at a smooth pace for even stitches. Practice controlling speed of machine on fabric scraps before starting on a finished quilt top.

Quilt following the needle punched paper design. You don't have to worry about getting off the line because the designs are organic and every flower can be a little different.

FREE MOTION GUIDE GRIP

Step 10. To make it easy to pop the paper from the stitches, slightly stretch the quilt on the bias. If the quilting is close together you will have to scratch the surface of the quilt with your finger nail to remove the paper.

Step 11. To sew straight lines, the Walking Foot works well. It can be used for cross hatching and stitching in the ditch. The machine will do the work and you will get perfect stitches.

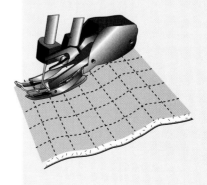

designed
and pieced by
Barbara Rezac

machine
quilted by
Linda Tailor

Appreciation to
Krause Publication
for permission to
duplicate pattern design

Applique the Madeira Way yardage
finished size 27 1/2" x 27 1/2"

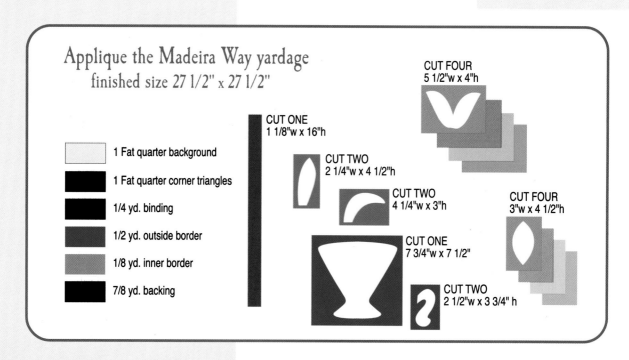

CUT FOUR
5 1/2"w x 4"h

CUT ONE
1 1/8"w x 16"h

1 Fat quarter background

1 Fat quarter corner triangles

1/4 yd. binding

1/2 yd. outside border

1/8 yd. inner border

7/8 yd. backing

CUT TWO
2 1/4"w x 4 1/2"h

CUT TWO
4 1/4"w x 3"h

CUT ONE
7 3/4"w x 7 1/2"

CUT FOUR
3"w x 4 1/2"h

CUT TWO
2 1/2"w x 3 3/4" h

Applique the Madeira Way

MADEIRA APPLIQUE

Barbara found this tulip pattern in a book written by Cindy Walter and Gayle Baker. In this block the patterns are duplicated from one side to another so Barbara could use the madeira applique method which comes from people doing heirloom sewing. This method gives us the look of needle-turned applique without having to do handwork. Making Madeira appliques is so easy to do with the water soluble basting thread.

Step 1. Cut a piece of "America Sews Fuse and Tear" stabilizer slightly smaller than a sheet of copy paper (about 8" x 10 1/2"). Press stabilizer to a sheet of copy paper. Be sure top edge of stabilizer that feeds into the copy machine is pressed well so it doesn't jam up your copy machine.

Step 2. Copy patterns on page 71 on to stabilizer and paper. Make sure copy machine prints on stabilizer and not on copy paper. Peel stabilizer off copy paper. It is a temporary stick and will peel off easily. You only need one of each shape because stabilizer will stick more than once. Cut independent shapes from stabilizer.

Step 3. Place fabric right sides together and press shiny side of pattern made on stabilizer to wrong side of top fabric. Fold fabric for vase in half and match fold to straight edge of vase. Press with iron.

Step 4. Thread machine with water soluble thread in top or bobbin (not both). Sew around pattern leaving a small area open for turning pattern to right side. Trim with pinking shears to eliminate bulk. **Don't forget to take wash-away thread out of machine when done!**

Step 5. Turn fabric to right side. A Fasturn tool is helpful. Use a blunt object to push out points. Finger press, then press with dry iron.

Step 6. Spray starch along seam line. Let spray be absorbed a couple minutes to dissolve thread. If thread doesn't dissolve, you may need to spritz again with water. Press until dry.

Step 7. Pull madeira apart and you will have two patterns mirror image of each other. There is only one vase because pattern was placed on fold. Edges of patterns have been turned to inside and are ready to apply to layout.

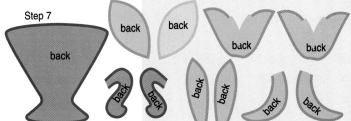

Step 8

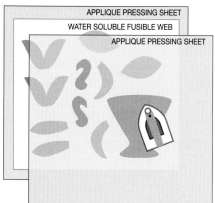

Step 8. Place Water Soluble Fusible Web on top of applique pressing sheet. Lay applique pieces right sides up on top of web. Place another applique pressing sheet on top and press with **dry iron** until web is fused to applique pieces. Peel applique pieces off pressing sheet. Trim any excess web with scissor so it doesn't get on iron. When pressing sheet is cool, excess residue will come off easily.

Step 9. Enlarge placement guide 400%. You can transfer the design to transparency film or copy paper on a copy machine. If using transparency film, hold transparency placement guide over top of fabric to find placement of pieces. If using copy paper, put paper placement guide under a 20" square of background fabric on a light table or a window. Trace pattern on to front of background fabric with fabric marking pencil.

Step 9

Step 10. Attach stems first. Cut a dark green strip for stems 1 1/8" x 16". Fold in half with wrong sides together. Press. Place over stem line on pattern. Move needle to right needle position and stitch with straight stitch along raw edges. Thread machine with Sulky invisible thread. Flip stem over raw edges and stitch along folded edge with blanket stitch (D heirloom stitches, stitch 46 on Husqvarna Viking Designers). You might want to adjust stitch width. Repeat to add all stems.

Step 10

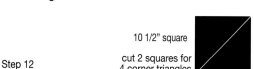

Step 11. Place remaining applique pieces following order on placement guide. Stitch in place with blanket stitch using invisible thread.

Step 12

10 1/2" square

cut 2 squares for 4 corner triangles

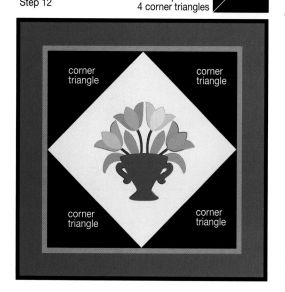

Step 11
PLACEMENT GUIDE
INCREASE 400%

Step 12. Trim applique block to a 14" square. Cut corner triangles and attach. Cut inner borders 1 1/4" wide and outer borders 3 1/2' wide. See pages 7-9 to add borders, make quilt sandwich, and bind. See quilt on page 66 for quilting ideas.

ACTUAL SIZE TEMPLATES

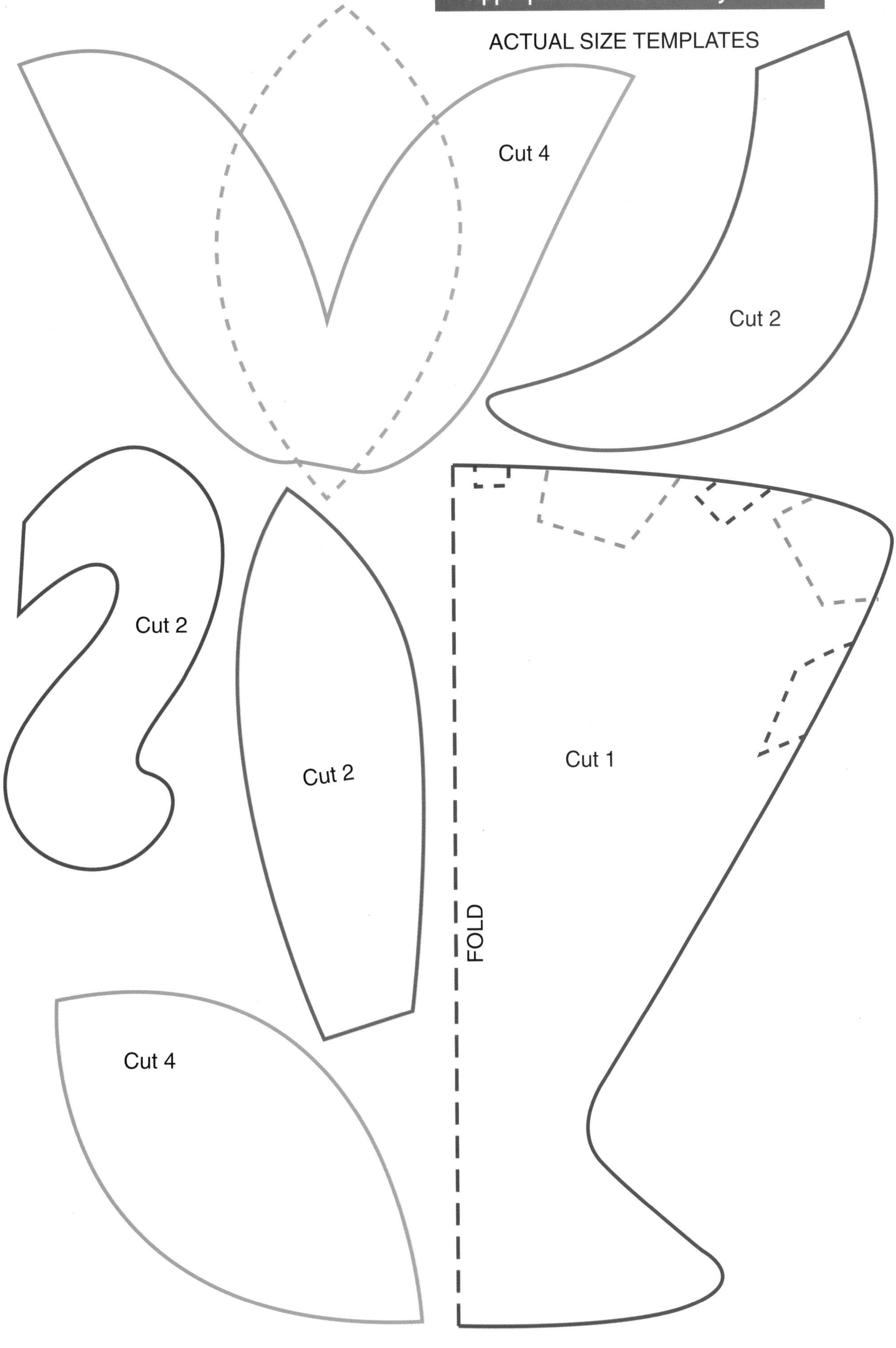

Cut 4

Cut 2

Cut 2

Cut 2

Cut 1

Cut 4

FOLD

Yardage Chart using 7 1/2" squares from scraps

# 7 1/2" SQUARES	YIELDS # BLOCKS	FINISHED SIZE
2	1	6" x 6"
8	4	12" x 12"
18	9	18" x 18"
32	16	24" x 24"
50	25	30" x 30"
72	36	36" x 36"
98	49	42" x 42"
128	64	48" x 48"
162	81	54" x 54'
200	100	60" x 60"
242	121	66" x 66"
288	144	72" x 72"
338	169	78" x 78"
392	196	84" x 84"
450	225	90' x 90"
512	256	96" x 96"
578	289	102" x 102"

designed
& pieced by
Cheryl Chan

machine quilted by
Jean Johnson

SELECTING FABRIC

Step 1. First choose a palette of scraps. Decide how far you want the range to go from light to dark and choose fabrics that have the same mood. The more fabrics you use, the easier it is to arrange the blocks without having same fabrics touch. You can use different lights or use all the same. You may also decide to use only two colors throughout the quilt. The Friendship Star block made in steps 1-12 can be combined with other nine-patch blocks (see steps 13 - 16), separated by plain blocks (step 17), or set between strips of sashing and corner stones (step 18).

Step 1

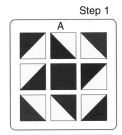

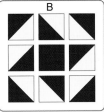

Step 2

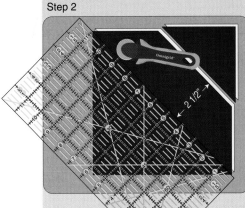

CUTTING INSTRUCTIONS

Step 2. Cut a 7 1/2" square from both light and dark fabric.

Step 3. Put squares together lining up edges. To save time, lay up to six squares together. Cut in half diagonally. Then cut 2 1/2" strips on both sides of center cut. Arrange strips alternating the colors. Repeat so you have two squares alike.

Step 4. Sew strips together with a scant 1/4" seam allowance. Repeat and sew second square. Finger press seams open. Press with an iron.

Step 3

Step 4

1/4"

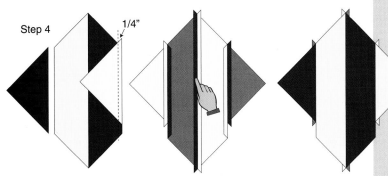

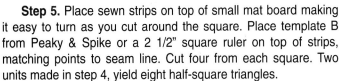

Step 5. Place sewn strips on top of small mat board making it easy to turn as you cut around the square. Place template B from Peaky & Spike or a 2 1/2" square ruler on top of strips, matching points to seam line. Cut four from each square. Two units made in step 4, yield eight half-square triangles.

If you are making a scrap quilt, you can either make each block from all the same prints or have each triangle from a different print. *See step 1.* If each half-square triangle is different, as in step 1A, you have to repeat steps 2-5 eight times to get enough variety for one block.

Step 5

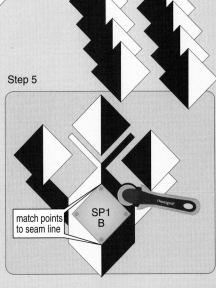

match points to seam line

SP1
B

Step 6

2 1/2" squares

Step 6. Cut a 2 1/2" square for center of each block. If all triangles are from the same fabric, the center should match. The center square can be different if all the points are different.

Step 7. Arrange eight half-square units to form a Friendship Star. Put a 2 1/2" square in the center.

Step 7

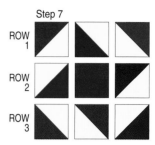

ROW 1
ROW 2
ROW 3

Step 8 **ROW 1**

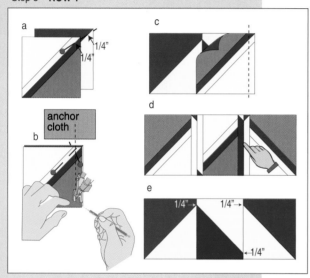

Step 8. Sew units together into rows with a scant 1/4' seam allowance (menu E stitch 1 on Husqvarna Viking Designers).

a. Row 1. Right sides together, connect two units. Make sure they are turned the right direction before sewing. To make a perfect intersection, insert pin 1/4" from edge on seam line through top and bottom. Leave this pin standing.

b. Insert another pin at the angle of the seam as shown and remove the standing pin. Do not back stitch at beginning or end of seam because it will be crossed over again. Start sewing on an anchor cloth. If you guide pieces in front of presser foot with a stiletto you won't have to worry about pieces scooting to one side at end of seam.

c. Repeat and add third unit to the row.

d. Finger press seam open before pressing with an iron.

e. The intersections should be 1/4" from edge.

Step 9 **ROW 2**

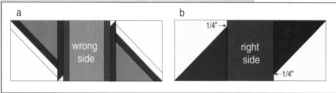

Step 9.

a. To make center row, connect a half-square unit on both sides of center square. Finger press seam open before pressing with an iron.

b. Intersections should be 1/4" from edge.

Step 10 **ROW 3**

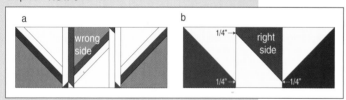

Step 10.

a. Make sure units are turned right direction before connecting them in third row. Repeat pinning instructions from step 8. Finger press seam open before pressing with an iron.

b. Intersections should be 1/4" from edge.

Step 11

Step 11. Right sides together, sew rows together. Insert pin 1/4" from outside edge at intersection indicated by arrow through top and bottom. Leave this pin standing. On both sides of standing pin, insert another pin to hold intersection in place. Remove standing pin before sewing seam.

Step 12

Step 12. Add the third row. Press seams open. Each block is a 6 1/2" square. Continue making blocks. Make sure all points on stars are turned in same direction. It is easy to get the points going in the opposite direction.

Making Alternating Nine-Patch Block

Step 13. Cut strips from light and dark scraps 2 1/2" wide for template B. Bifold strips on a small mat board so it is easier to turn your work as you cut around the template. Place template B on top of strips and cut number of pieces needed. Each nine-patch has five dark and four light squares.

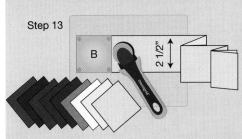

Step 13

Step 14

a. Place a light and dark A right sides together. Match corners and sew with a scant 1/4" seam allowance (menu E stitch 1 on Husqvarna Viking Designers). Do not back stitch at either end of seam.

Step 14

a

match corners

b. Continue connecting squares alternating light and dark fabrics as shown. Make three rows. Finger press seams open before pressing with an iron.

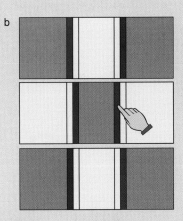

b

c. Place two rows right sides together. Insert a pin 1/4" from outside edge on seam line through top and bottom. Leave this pin standing.

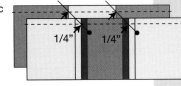

c

1/4"   1/4"

d. On both sides of standing pin, insert another pin to hold intersection in place. Remove standing pin. Do not back stitch when sewing seam.

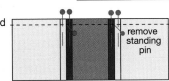

d

remove standing pin

e. Repeat and add third row. Press seams open. Each block is a 6 1/2" square.

e

Step 15. Right sides together, place a Friendship Star block on top of a Nine-patch block so intersections you want to sew over are visible. Insert a pin 1/4" from the edge on seam line through top and bottom. Leave this pin standing. Insert another pin on both sides of the standing pin. Sew seam. Press seam open. The quilt size is determined by the number of blocks made.

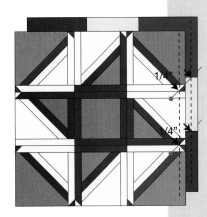

1/4"

1/4"

2Step 16. This Nine-Patch is another good alternate block. Each corner half-square triangle has a different color. The light half-square triangles and squares can all be different or all from the same light fabric.

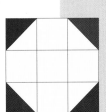

Step 17. Separating the Friendship Stars with a plain square gives you a nice area for quilting.

Step 18. Sashing and corner stones separate these Friendship Star blocks.

Step 19. Add one or two borders to your quilt after you have connected the blocks into your favorite style. The inside border is usually cut 1 1/2" - 2" wide. The outside border is cut 5" - 6" wide. See page 7 for instructions to attach borders. See page 8 to make quilt sandwich.

The diagram below shows how my quilt is going to be quilted.
See page 9 for binding instructions.

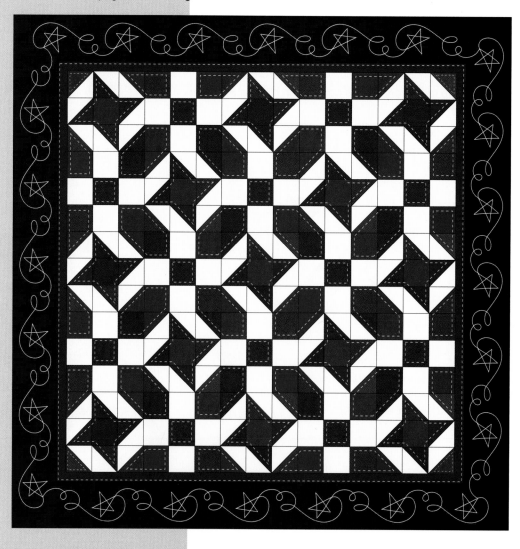

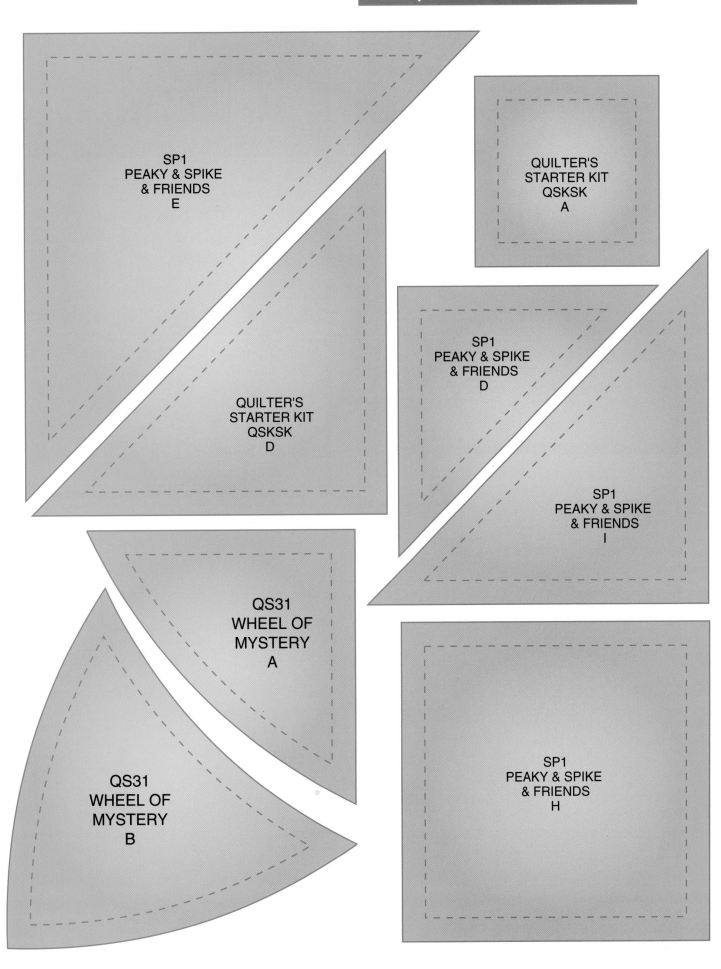

SP1
PEAKY & SPIKE
& FRIENDS
E

QUILTER'S
STARTER KIT
QSKSK
A

QUILTER'S
STARTER KIT
QSKSK
D

SP1
PEAKY & SPIKE
& FRIENDS
D

SP1
PEAKY & SPIKE
& FRIENDS
I

QS31
WHEEL OF
MYSTERY
A

QS31
WHEEL OF
MYSTERY
B

SP1
PEAKY & SPIKE
& FRIENDS
H

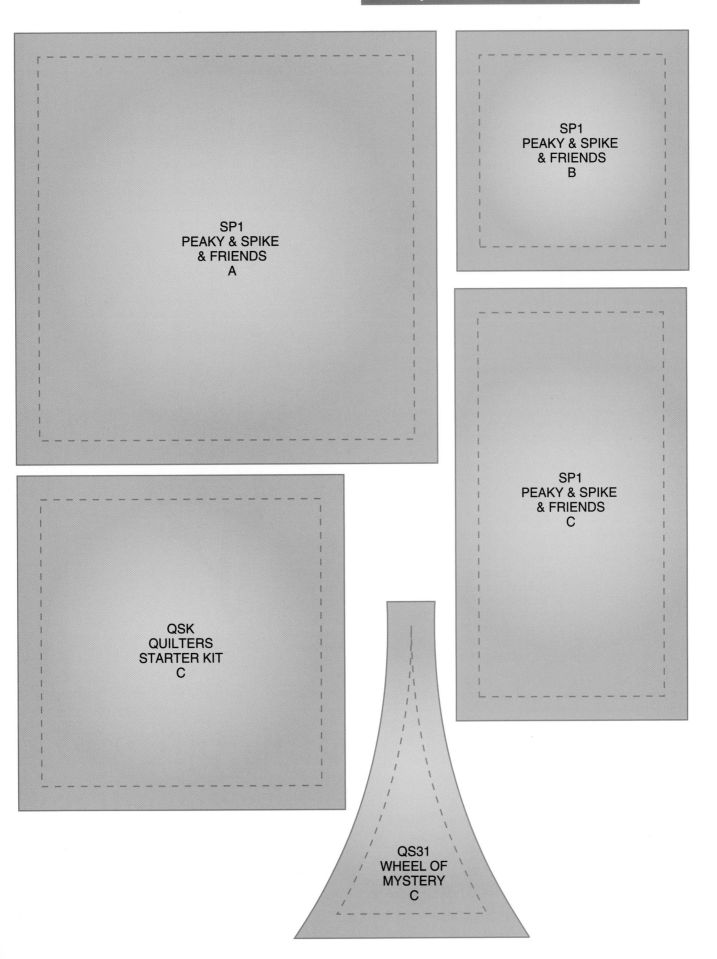

SP1
PEAKY & SPIKE
& FRIENDS
A

SP1
PEAKY & SPIKE
& FRIENDS
B

SP1
PEAKY & SPIKE
& FRIENDS
C

QSK
QUILTERS
STARTER KIT
C

QS31
WHEEL OF
MYSTERY
C

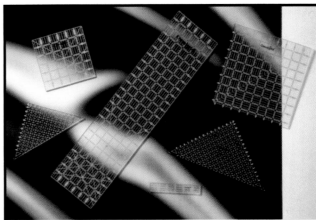